CW00401565

FIVE BIG

Concepts That Shape Our Culture

by Mal Fletcher

'I believe in Christianity as I believe that the Sun has risen:
not only because I see it, but because by it
I see everything else.'

C. S. Lewis

'The Christian ideal has not been tried and found wanting;
it has been found difficult and left untried.'

G. K. Chesterton

Next Wave International™

Published by Next Wave International™
Visit our website at www.nextwaveonline.com

ISBN 978-0-9803956-1-7

1. Cultural Studies   2. Christian Apologetics 3. Leadership

Unless otherwise stated, Scripture quotations are from the New International Version of the Bible, copyright 1973, 1978 and 1984 by International Bible Society.

Cover Art: Jon Smethurst, Kingdom Faith
Layout: Next Wave International
Printed in the UK.

Next Wave International™
Post: 155 Regents Park Road,
London, NW1 8BB, UK
office@nextwaveonline.com

And

Next Wave International™
PO Box 106, Reynella S.A., 5161, Australia
gary@nextwaveonline.com

FIVE BIG IDEAS

Concepts That Shape Our Culture

by Mal Fletcher

Next Wave International™

INTRODUCTION
WHAT WERE THEY THINKING?!

Did you ever see a person do or say something and ask: 'What on earth were they *thinking* when they did that!?'

That thought crosses my mind every time I visit an airport – which is quite frequently. I see the word 'terminal' written above the main airport building and think, 'Why on earth would anyone use that word in *this* place!?' I mean, airline passengers are about to trust their lives to a thin tube of metal, which flies at 30,000 feet and is controlled mainly by microchips. The last thing they want to read before they hurtle into the sky is a word that literally means 'ending in death'.

Let's face it, there are times when people just don't seem to be thinking straight – or thinking at all! You've probably come across people who act as if they've never entertained a thought in their lives. Ours is a highly emotive culture which often seems to encourage a preoccupation with feelings over ideas. Yet people *do* think and they act accordingly, living out their worldview, their concept of what is good, normal and acceptable.

This is why the apostle Paul reminded his protégé Timothy that: '[God] wishes all men to be saved and increasingly to perceive and recognise and discern and know precisely and correctly the divine truth' (1 Timothy 2:4, *Amplified Version*). To rise above the culture in which we live, to influence it more than it impacts us, we must become people who function on more than emotion. We must learn to nurture and develop ideas. The famed Christian apologist C. S. Lewis said that we need good philosophy if only to answer all the bad philosophy that's going around. The same is true of ideas generally: we need godly ideas – ideas that line up with our revelation of who God is – to overcome the ungodly ideas that often drive modern living.

Perhaps that was part of Jesus' thinking when he said that the greatest of all commandments is to: 'Love the Lord your God with all your heart and with all your soul and with all your mind and with all your strength' (Mark 12:30). The kingdom of God's love is born first in our spirit (the 'heart'); then it affects our emotions, passions and motivations (the 'soul'). It must then change our thinking (our 'mind') so that it can rightly affect our actions (our 'strength'). Some Christians want to skip a step in this process. They want to love God with their heart, then experience him in their emotions and then immediately see the benefits in their lifestyle. Because they haven't engaged their mind in the process of loving God and serving him, they become indecisive, unreliable and frustrated.

Let me ask you one simple but very important question: what are you thinking? What ideas are driving your life? What concepts are pushing you forward into your future – and helping to create that future?

Use It Or Lose It

We live in an increasingly automated world, where machines run complex processes without human intervention. In this world of super-miniature microchips, radio frequency ID tags (RFIDs) and nanotechnology, it's easy to imagine a time when machines will run everything in our lives. Some futurists have predicted – only half-jokingly – that airplanes of the future will feature a cockpit crew that consists of just one pilot and a dog. The pilot's job will be to feed the dog. The dog's role will be to bite the pilot if he tries to touch anything! Despite predictions like that, the human mind will continue to be, as it is today, one of the world's truly great resources.

Alzheimer's disease is the most common form of senile dementia. The most common early symptom is a loss of short-term memory, making people appear quite forgetful. As the disorder progresses, the brain suffers impairment in areas of language, skilled movement, recognition and decision-making.

Nobody knows the ultimate cause of the disease – though genetic factors are known to play a part. What is known is that rates of Alzheimer's are 14 times higher among illiterate people with no education than among those who had at least five year's education. The brain needs exercise if it is to grow and stay healthy. Without being trite, we can say that when it comes to your mind, if you don't use it you'll lose it!

We need to be continually aware of the ideas that shape our values and behaviour. The Bible suggests that this may be especially true in our generation. Paul warned his disciple Timothy of a time 'in the last days' when people would be 'forever inquiring and getting information, but ... never able to arrive at a recognition and knowledge of the truth' (2 Timothy 3:7).

There are at least five big ideas that lie behind much of the activity in our culture today. Though people seldom dwell on them consciously or deliberately, these ideas shape their responses to the big questions of life. Psychologists talk about 'gestalt', a collection of symbols that our brain uses to create a unified concept or pattern, a picture of reality. When a small child looks up and sees a cloud, he might see a pattern there; perhaps a pony, or a flower. The brain identifies new stimuli with patterns it already recognises.

The ideas we're about to discuss have helped to shape the pattern of thinking of millions of people across the world. As we'll see, these ideas are quite different from those that underpin the rising kingdom of God, the kingdom Jesus announced and personified. In fact, each of these ideas finds its counterpoint in the Christian Scriptures. If Christians are to influence the popular culture more than it influences them, they must be familiar with these potent concepts and answer them with godly alternatives. If you're determined to shape your environment more than it shapes you, read on...

IDEA #1

TECHNOLOGICAL PRAGMATISM
IF SOMETHING WORKS, IT MUST BE GOOD

One hundred years ago, toward the end of the Industrial Revolution, people gladly invited technology into their homes. New tools such as washing machines, sewing machines and refrigerators made domestic life more comfortable. At the same time, people were awestruck by the new technologies of transportation which freed them from the tyranny of distance. They also made friends with the new technologies they encountered in the workplace.

For some, though, all this change represented a threat to human wellbeing. Luddite-types predicted that machines would quickly take over all the jobs traditionally done by human beings. They predicted that modern methods of transportation would eventually destroy the fabric of society, because people speeding from place to place would have little time for conversation.

You and I have grown up thinking of these technologies as commonplace. In many cases, we only take notice of them when they're *not* working. Where would we be without our PDA phones, laptops, palmtops and mp3/mp4 players? For us, technology is simply a fact of life. However, there's been a subtle corollary to our acceptance of technology. As we've opened our lives to it, we've gradually accepted without question a line of thought that basically says, 'if something works, it must be good'. This is technological pragmatism. It measures the moral rightness of something according to whether it performs a function or meets a need.

Technology is the practical outworking or manifestation of scientific discovery. Science 'discovers' and technology turns the discovery into something we can use. 'From Newton onwards,' writes Bryan Appleyard, 'science poured out its laws and technology turned them into steam engines, factories, cars and rockets.'[1] In the end, he says, the big claim to fame of any new technology is that 'it works' - it does something we've never been able to do before.

However, when we start to accept technologies mainly – even solely – on the basis of their utility, we're setting ourselves up for trouble, as we'll see in a moment.

Most of us have taken on the technological pragmatist line of thinking without being aware of it. We've done that for two reasons; firstly, because we're a little overwhelmed by the pace of change in our lives. In his seminal work *Future Shock*, Alvin Toffler warned of what he called a 'roaring current of change' which would leave people feeling increasingly disoriented and stressed. This book, written in the 1970s, proved to be prophetic, with the fulfilment of its predictions taking place in our time. People *are* feeling pressurized by the speed of change; so much so that when radical new technologies break into the public consciousness, many people simply throw up their hands and say, 'Hey, I've got too much going on already to think about the rights and wrongs of this thing. *Just do it…*'

Secondly, technology is, for most of us, more of a friend than a foe. As I noted in *The Church of 2020,* 'We live in a world where there are now more microprocessors than people. The power of PCs has been doubling every 18 months for many years. At that rate it means we will see machines in 2024 with processors that are 10,000 times more powerful than the fastest chips we have today. [We can] expect breakthroughs with nanotechnology within 20 years, allowing chips to shrink massively to microscopic levels.'[2] None of this surprises or worries us – we've made friends with technology; we've learned to think that all technology is helpful.

Playing With The Building Blocks

Technology makes it easier for us to buy and sell, to bank, to be entertained and to communicate with one another. It allows the fast exchange of ideas and the opportunity to express our creativity. Unlike our grandparents and great-grandparents, we're comfortable using technology in the home, in transportation and at work. What's new in our time is that we're inviting technology into our bodies.

We're standing on the threshold of a whole new era in science. The discoveries that lay just around the next corner will probably dwarf all the great developments of the last century. The big technologies of this age could change forever the very makeup of the human being.

For example, in much of the West, laws currently prohibit human cloning and limit stem cell research, yet some scientists are working on technologies that will dramatically influence human reproduction. Supporters of human genetic engineering point to benefits that have already come through research and development. For example, since IVF treatments were launched in the late 1970s, they have helped thousands of couples to become parents for the first time. On the back of this, science is quickly learning how to screen embryos against genetic defects and hereditary diseases.

In the last 10 years, scientists have been doing a lot of work with germline genetic engineering. Working with animal embryos, researchers add or subtract sections of their DNA to produce particular outcomes. The goal, of course, is to do the same with people, to shape human characteristics that are affected by our genes, such as intelligence, sporting ability and even emotional stability.

For all the hype surrounding these developments, many philosophers and theologians question whether advances in scientific knowledge *always* lead to a better society. Are scientific progress and human advancement *really* one and the same thing?

Anthropologists want to know what these new technologies will mean for families and communities. In some nations, many female babies are aborted for cultural reasons, such as the fact that parents must pay a high dowry price to marry off their female children. As a result, there's a huge imbalance between the male and female populations in these nations. What will happen within these populations if people are able to genetically engineer the sex of their children?

Some authorities warn that genetic selection techniques may lead to a new apartheid. Genetically enhanced people may one day be separated from their natural-born counterparts and given special privileges – as in the movie *Gattaca*. DNA printouts may one day become a central part of every job-seeker's CV. We have enough alienation in our world as it is, without inventing more.

Lawmakers will face major dilemmas. For example, does one partner in a marriage have the right to use the other's genetic material, after the relationship has ended? Can a woman use her dead husband's frozen sperm? These questions are already before our courts, but they are just a taste of the legal puzzles to come. Will marriage partners try to stop one another from using embryonic gene treatments? Will children sue their biological parents for not giving them a better gene structure? The mind boggles!

Being a parent is already a demanding business; just imagine how stressful it will be in a world of 'designer babies', where we struggle to keep up with the genetically modified Joneses. Most of us have enough trouble choosing the colour of our next car. How will we cope with choices that will affect our child's personality or intelligence? And what happens when child number two or three is on the way and new genetic features become available? Will we inject upgrade 'patches' into our older kids, or just learn to say, 'Why can't you be more like your *younger* brother?'

Science Is Not Value Free

As we let the hi-tech genie emerge even more from his bottle – especially in areas like genetics – our technological capacity is racing ahead of our ethics. The problem is not with the science itself – to quote the old *Six Million Dollar Man* TV series, 'We have the technology…' The challenge we face is with the moral, ethical and practical consequences of *using* our knowledge.

It's one thing to be *able* to do something and quite another to acknowledge the moral consequences of carrying it out. Alexander Solzhenitsyn, the great Russian novelist and moralist, said: 'All the celebrated technological achievements of progress, including the conquest of outer space, do not redeem the twentieth century's moral poverty.'[3]

Some people will say, 'Pure science is value free; we shouldn't hold scientists responsible for how their knowledge is used.' Albert Einstein would disagree. His simple equation $E=MC^2$ provided the basis for the building of the atom bomb. Yet Einstein set up an annual meeting for scientists who wanted to discuss the dangers of nuclear weapons. He believed that scientists must take moral responsibility for their discoveries.

The kind of pragmatism that rules much of science today says, 'If a thing can be done, it should be done – even if we haven't shown how it may pan out in the long run.' But one of the things that makes us human, setting us apart from other creatures, is that we can decide not to do something we are capable of doing. Our morality is part of what defines us and morality is all about the choices we make between what we *could* do and what we *should* do.

How Do You Measure Morality?

Obviously, we can't stop the forward march of human knowledge. We wouldn't want to. Curiosity is what leads us to new frontiers. But we *must* think responsibly about where new technologies might take us. We can't possibly know how the technological decisions we make today will shape future generations.

The French philosopher Jacques Ellul saw the potential dangers. 'We build faster and faster machines,' he wrote, 'to take us absolutely nowhere.' He warned that, if we're not watchful, the 'values of the machine' – his term for technological pragmatism – would absorb us, becoming an inherent part of who we are and threatening both our spirituality and humanity.

Technological pragmatism ultimately leans heavily upon Darwin's evolutionary theory. If we apply the notion of species advancement through natural selection to the entire human condition, we end up with the notion that whatever advances the human climb up the evolutionary chain must be good. In 1876, Darwin wrote in his *Autobiography*: 'A man who has no assured ... belief in the existence of a personal God or of a future existence with retribution and reward, can have for his rule of life ... only to follow those impulses and instincts which are the strongest or which seemed to him the best ones.' Yet even he saw the weakness in this kind of thinking: 'The horrid doubt always arises whether the convictions of men's mind, which has developed from the mind of the lower animals, are of any value or at all trustworthy. Would anyone trust the conviction of a monkey's mind, if there are any convictions in such a mind?'

The Bible gives us a very different measure for our standard of morality and a motive for living by it: 'I am the LORD your God; consecrate yourselves and be holy, because I am holy' (Leviticus 11:44). In the biblical worldview, the moral rightness of something is ultimately based not on whether or not it seems to work, or whether it is convenient, but on how it lines up with the revealed nature and character of God. When it comes to deciding what's right, pragmatism must be tempered with revelation. And our response to revelation must be that we consecrate ourselves, setting ourselves apart from the kinds of people we might have become had God not shown himself to us.

In most Old Testament, bronze-age societies, the manufacture, buying and selling of idols was big business. People bought images of their favourite gods because they seemed to add practical benefits to everyday life. There were idols for protection, health and virility and idols to help your crops grow. In fact, many cultures had pocket-sized gods to cover just about every area of human activity. Idols were commonplace even, it must be said, in Israel, where divine injunctions forbade them from keeping idols. Why were idols forbidden in Israel? Is it because God is a cultural Philistine who can't appreciate the finer points of sculpture? No, there were two reasons for it.

Firstly, when you make an idol to represent God you freeze your revelation of Him; you say to yourself, 'this is all God can ever be for me – nothing more than this'.

Imagine that you've just married. On your bedside table you have a wonderful photograph of your partner. One day, shortly after the honeymoon, you wake up and say to your partner, 'You can leave now if you like. I don't need you any more; I've got this great photo of you.' Ridiculous? Yes – you can't build a relationship with a photograph, which is just an image frozen in time. Relationship requires an ongoing process of revelation, each party revealing their innermost thoughts, hopes and hurts over time. This is true of all human relationships, but even more so of relationship with God.

I recently conducted a TV interview with my good friend, author and teacher Winkie Pratney. For more than forty years, Winkie has travelled the globe speaking to young adults in festivals, universities, conferences and churches. He is, to my mind, one of the Christian world's leading social researchers – and happens also to be an authority on historic revivals, which is a great mix. In our interview, Winkie made this interesting point: 'You can't have a digital download from an infinite transmitter to a finite receptor.'

I was intrigued. He explained that if God were to reveal himself *completely* to any one of us, we'd be dead in a nanosecond. Think about it: how can our brain matter, as wonderful as it is, possibly take in the enormity of the One who made the universe – and, if you believe the science journals, possibly other universes – with a word? 'So,' Winkie continued, 'God has to reveal himself to us, as the Scripture puts it, "line upon line, precept upon precept".'[4]

A relationship with God requires progressive revelation. We can't know him if we limit our understanding to a fixed image based on past experience. The Shorter Westminster Catechism says that 'man's chief end is to glorify God, and to enjoy him forever.' Relationship with God is the primary reason for our creation. It is also the only means by which we can become all that we were designed to be.

In the Christian worldview, we are not monkeys who got lucky or gorillas that had a good hair day. We are each the deliberate creation of a wise, benevolent and purposeful God who made us for a reason. Unlike any of the other creatures on God's amazing Earth, we were made in his special likeness. This means that we possess certain attributes that mark us out as God's special favourites. Among these is our ability to choose between right and wrong; to act not merely on the basis of instinct, survival or even social benefit, but according to a sense of morality.

Another of our special characteristics is a quest for immortality, a drive for heroism. No other creature possesses that same urge. You don't find gorillas jumping out of planes from thirty thousand feet with a parachute. You don't find dogs running for Olympic glory. Human beings alone possess an urge to push the boundaries of self-expression. We are the only creatures who are eager to achieve something that will live on when we're gone.

Being made in God's image also means that we were intended to follow his example. We are not God, but were intended to learn to be like him, in the same way that a child will admire and seek to emulate his or her parents. When my son Grant was very young, he would watch me speaking on stage in large auditoriums, or playing with my band, and when he got home he'd set up his own stage on his bed, complete with pretend lighting cans and sound systems. It's healthy for kids to want to be like their parents – provided mum and dad are trying to do the right things.

It's even healthier for people to try to act like their heavenly Father. We were made in God's image, with an innate desire to grow up to be like him. That, in essence, is what the Bible means by the word 'righteousness': to act in line with, or in accord with, God's way of thinking and behaving, as it has been revealed to us in the Bible – and especially through the person of Jesus Christ. If we cease to grow in our understanding of who God is and what he is like, says the apostle Paul, our thinking becomes 'futile' and our hearts are 'darkened' – another version says we trivialise ourselves (Romans 1:21). To save us from that God says, 'Be holy as I am holy; set your standards according to what you learn of me.'

When we stop growing in our revelation of God, we stop progressing in our understanding of what is good in life. God is the *essence* of all that is good. God doesn't just act truly, he is absolute truth. He doesn't merely behave fairly; he is the measure of justice itself. He doesn't only feel love, he *is* love! If we take God out of the world, we create a moral black hole that sucks all moral light into itself and has us accepting every new theory that comes along. As one wise man put it, 'When a man stops believing in God, he doesn't believe in nothing, he believes in anything.'

Taking God out of our frame of reference is akin to trying to read a map without knowing which way is north, or using a compass from which the magnet's been removed. It's dangerous to construct our measure of goodness on anything other than the unchanging purity of God's character.

In contemporary culture, we no longer take the word of authority figures at face value. In fact, we're more likely to question people like politicians and police personnel simply because they *are* authority figures. Very often, there are only two groups of people we'll listen to without asking too many questions: media personalities and scientists. For some reason, we've come to believe that the TV camera doesn't lie; that everything the box says is worth serious consideration simply because it's on the box. Malcolm Muggeridge, the pioneer BBC TV journalist and commentator, said: 'Not only can the camera lie, it always lies.'[5] In the process of transporting events via media, decisions are made at every stage as to what should be included and what should be left out. We're never really getting the complete picture.

Scientists often enjoy a similar level of respect. Some scientists like to talk as if they're making infallible pronouncements which we should take on face value. But they can't possibly predict the future effects of their technologies, especially when things are moving as quickly as they are in disciplines like genetics. We honestly have no way of knowing how the genetic changes we make today will play out in the world of our children's children. We're making decisions that will affect many generations to come. Can we – should we – accept that kind of responsibility?

In a sense, the Bible is God's satellite navigation system. If we approach it with a hungry heart, it can lift us above our existential struggles and show us the safest route to our ultimate destination – and the best sights to see along the way. It is not God's intention to stifle our curiosity or creativity. He requires, though, that we measure our actions or intentions against his holiness and goodness, rather than human expediency alone. It's the only safe route for us and for our world.

[1] *Understanding The Present: Science and the Soul of Modern Man*, Bryan Appleyard (Pan Books 1992), p. 69.

[2] *The Church of 2020,* Mal Fletcher (Next Wave International, 2006), p.12.

[3] Quoted in *Wild Hope,* Tom Sine (Monarch, 1991), p. 169.

[4] *Mal Fletcher Speaks with Winkie Pratney* (Next Wave Media, 2007). See the interview at nextwaveonline.com.

[5] *Christ and the Media*, Malcolm Muggeridge, (Regent College Publishing, 2003), p. 30.

IDEA #2

MORAL RELATIVISM
FREEDOM MEANS DOING AS I PLEASE

One historian has said, 'We live in an age of uncertainty about everything.' Ours is a world of incredible complexity, where the only certainty is change itself.

This is the age of 'whatever', which is not so much a cry for revolution as a sigh of resignation. Given the endless stream of life decisions we face every day, people often respond to the problems of the world with cynicism and apathy. 'I can't decide what's right for you,' they say, 'and I don't really want to think about it, so just do *whatever…*'

For centuries, individuals, families and whole nations gained strength from a belief in absolutes; a conviction that some things are universally right and others are universally wrong. People accepted this idea for several reasons. First of all, they knew that certain basic absolutes were clearly outlined in religious texts such as the Bible. Injunctions against murder, theft, adultery and dishonesty were fundamental to peoples' largely religious worldview.

In fact, relativism really only took hold in the West when people began to reject Christianity's teachings about the existence of God. If there is no God, moral values are simply the products of socio-biological evolution. Philosopher Michael Ruse says: 'Morality is a biological adaptation no less than our heads and feet and teeth.' Morality, he adds, 'is just an aid to survival and reproduction… any deeper meaning is illusory.'[1]

Alternatively, if there is no God, morality is a matter of personal taste. So, to say that killing innocent children is wrong would be the same as saying, 'I don't much like the killing of innocent children.' It would be nothing more than a statement of subjective preference. Yet, most people would argue against such an act on the basis that it offends more than mere personal taste; it is morally and universally wrong.

Traditionally, people also accepted the existence of universal moral absolutes because human experience seemed to bear this out. Murder is never right; it destroys the lives not only of its victims, but of family members and friends – not to mention the perpetrators. Theft always brings loss and heartache. Adultery always gives birth to anger, disillusionment and distrust, damaging the lives of individuals and families. We might try to put a liberal spin on them, but certain types of behaviour always lead to negative consequences.

Thirdly, people accepted the notion of absolute right and wrong because they sensed the presence of an in-built witness to the truth of these absolutes; something commonly called conscience. Many liberals today will talk about the need to adhere to the dictates of 'social conscience', by which they mean the sense of right and wrong which is shared by most of the people in a community. However, the notion that there can be a collective conscience without an individual one is nonsense. Social conscience is only a collective reflection of the deeply held moral beliefs of individual people.

Rewind To The Present

In our time, many people scoff at moral absolutes. They replace them with less certain things - like pragmatism and image. As we've seen, pragmatism says, 'If a thing can be done, it should be done, even if we haven't thought through the consequences.' Image says, 'The appearance is more important than the reality; if we like the way things look, we won't bother to check behind the mask.'

Ironically, when we reject absolutes, we water down the concept of tolerance. Societies that have been strongly influenced by Christianity have usually been tolerant societies. Tolerance recognises that people have a right to make certain choices, even if their choices are unhealthy. Traditionally, a tolerant attitude might have said to someone, 'You can believe that if you want to, but it's wrong.' Nowadays we have a less gutsy kind of tolerance; it says, 'You can believe anything you want to, because *nothing* is wrong.'

Pragmatism, image and this new form of tolerance are built on relativism. Relativism claims that there is no such thing as eternal, objective truth; there's no truth which is true for everyone, at all times. It says that whether an action is moral or not depends entirely on the context. Relativism has given birth to a strange child called political correctness. Many people today have only one moral goal: not to offend anyone else. Political correctness says, 'You can call anything true, as long as you don't insist that it is *the* truth for everyone.'

Today, the concepts of conscience and absolute truth are often viewed as quaint throw-backs to less enlightened times, or as psychologically damaging ideas that are promoted by religious authorities who hunger for power.

As the name suggests, a relativistic worldview insists that morals are relative rather than fixed; that no individual or authority has the right to prescribe what is proper for other people. Standards of morality and ethics are in a constant state of flux, changing according to the existential situation. What is an appropriate response in one circumstance may be totally inappropriate in another. There are no ultimate standards against which we can or should measure human morality – or, at least none that rely on anything more than pragmatism. If we do elevate certain standards of behaviour over others, it is only because we collectively agree that they work better than others – both for individuals and for society as a whole.

Moral relativism says: 'I am a free agent; no one can tell me what I should or should not do. I answer to nobody but myself.' It's a school of thought often described as 'situation ethic'. 'My circumstance,' it says, 'will determine what is right for me.'

People often associate the growth of situation ethic as a cultural norm with the rise of the Baby Boom generation in the 1950s, 60s and 70s – though it actually has a much longer pedigree. 'Do your own thing' became a mantra among the Boomer hippies and flower children who featured so strongly in the so-called 'summer of love'. From there it gradually spread to become a part of the wider youth culture and then mainstream Western culture. The movies, TV and music of the time were quick to use this cliché to summarise the aspirations of an entire generation. The truth is, though, that many Boomers never bought into this philosophy at all.

While the flower power age gave rise to drug-induced psychedelia, sexual experimentation and a renewed interest in eastern mysticism, it also produced one of the greatest revivals of Christian faith in modern times, the so-called 'Jesus movement'. Like their 'free-love' contemporaries, these young people rebelled against the staid traditions of their parents' Silent Generation, but in a completely different way.

These 'Jesus people', as they branded themselves, were just as 'counter-culture' as their hippie peers but they challenged the dead, institutional religion and corrupt politics of mainstream culture with a radical return to the teachings of Christ, rather than the pursuit of eastern gurus and political anarchists. Politically, they became involved in issues of justice and equality because they believed in God's compassionate nature and righteous character, rather than out of disillusionment with human governments.

For more than forty years, Boomers have played a large part in shaping the cultural mores of Western societies. In fact, through the spread of Western communication technologies, they have helped to shape values across the world. Boomer-directed movies and Boomer-produced music have carried with them a largely fluid approach to morality and ethics. During the Boomer cultural reign, relativism has pervaded mainstream culture. It has had forty years or more to prove its worth, so what is its record, what has it produced?

The Record Of Relativism

In the West, moral relativism has led societies down a road to insecurity, alienation and conflict. During its time at the top, divorce rates have soared and many children have lost the nurturing of a stable home. In many nations, crime has increased out of all proportion to the growth in populations. Western prisons are filling up or full, and court back-logs are growing as the justice system struggles to keep up with the demands on its services.

Meanwhile, many criminals try to blame someone else for their faults and are often encouraged to do so by well-meaning but misguided social workers and mental health experts. At the same time, many of society's once trusted institutions have become the targets of greater public cynicism than ever before. The public perception – and it's not always a fair one – is that politicians and other public officials are led by self-interest rather than a sense of public duty, while a reliance on spin and focus groups has replaced honest and courageous leadership at the top.

In *Christ and the Media,* Malcolm Muggeridge wondered whether archaeologists sifting through the debris of our lifetime might not find a society that 'destroyed itself ... in the fond expectation that it was reforming itself.'[2] In the words of song-writer Larry Norman, we may well be 'walking backwards down the stairs, trying to get higher.'

In October 2006, British newspapers reported that government ministers were changing direction in their approach to dealing with an extremely high rate of teen pregnancies. In the past, UK government agencies encouraged school nurses to hand out morning-after pills and distribute explicit sex guides, teaching kids how to use condoms. The latest strategy, though, involved a complete turn around, with teens being encouraged to abstain from sexual activity at least until they're over 16 years of age.

The 'Leave it Till Later' campaign was trumpeted – as are all government initiatives – as something fresh and revolutionary. Apparently, the government had spent more than £163 million since 1998 trying to tackle teen pregnancy, with only limited success. However, this 'new' approach was not as novel as it made out. It followed on the heels of the 'Silver Ring Thing' initiative in the US and Britain, where 20,000 teens vowed to remain virgins until marriage.[3]

This project, launched by concerned Christian parents, avoids talking to teens about contraception, believing that doing so sends out a conflicting message. The group's statistics suggest that teaching kids how to say 'no' to sex offers a much higher success rate than offering them contraceptives. Where relativism fails miserably, righteousness succeeds.

Offering young people nothing more than contraceptives is simply an admission of defeat and an insult to their resilience and independence. All too often, we've assumed that just because their parents are too weak to say 'no' to something, the kids are going to be the same. Or we've assumed that peer pressure can only work in one direction, invariably pulling kids down. If we're willing to help them, young people can change their own culture so that peer pressure works in a positive direction, urging kids to be the best they can be.

After years of messing around with liberal approaches based upon moral relativism and situation ethic, the British government had to admit that they did not work. Sadly, millions of young lives were negatively affected in the years it took them to discover – or admit – that fact.

Reality Anybody?

If you want to witness the dangers of letting moral relativism reign supreme, you need look no further than your TV.

Without a doubt, TV has brought a great deal of good into our lives. Part of my work is as a TV producer and presenter – and I'm an avid TV watcher – so I fully appreciate the power of this unique medium to entertain and to shape opinions. Sadly, TV's potency has often been used for less than noble ends, especially in this age of increasing media competitiveness. Traditional media platforms are fragmenting in the wake of the Internet and mobile technology revolutions. Many broadcasters – or 'content providers' – are struggling to fill the hours of programming needed across all the new platforms, which means a loss of quality.

'Fictional good is boring and flat,' said one writer, 'while fictional evil is varied, intriguing, attractive and full of charm.'[4] For some reason, too, fictional good appears 'old-hat', while fictional evil appears up-to-date and trendy.

I asked the Archbishop of Canterbury, Dr. Rowan Williams, what he would say to young adults who, working in the media, found that they couldn't express their worldview in their work because of the pressure to be politically correct. He said: 'I don't ask the media to take us back to a bygone age when the church had political power. But I do ask them not to *disadvantage* us just *because* we are part of the tradition, the history of the culture.' This is perhaps one reason why we don't see more contemporary programming that reflects a Christian worldview – for some people, representing virtues like goodness just seems so 'last century'!

All too often, TV schedules are filled with programmes that play on cheap violence, sexual promiscuity and moral manipulation to attract an audience. Take, for example, some examples of the so-called reality TV genre. (I say 'so-called' because if some of these programmes represent your idea of reality, you probably need to get out of the house more often!)

In early 2007, much of Europe was shocked to hear about the impending broadcast of a new show in the *Big Brother* mould, which was entitled *The Big Donor Show*. Produced in the Netherlands, this one-off programme was to be built around three contestants who would compete, in front of a prime-time audience, for the prize of a life-saving kidney operation.

A terminally ill cancer patient, aged 37, had apparently agreed to donate a healthy kidney. She said that her decision to take part in the programme was based on a desire to avoid the anonymity normally associate with organ donation; she wanted to meet the recipient of her kidney. The producers defended the programme saying that the contestants were being given a much higher chance of receiving a kidney than they would have had if they went through normal channels. In fact, they said, the show would perform a valuable public service by raising awareness of an important health issue. In fact, they were turning a serious medical matter, organ donation, into a game-show contest, or worse, a circus.

In the end, *The Big Donor Show* turned out to be an elaborate hoax. The programme went to air, but the 'donor' turned out to be an actress and all of the contestants – genuine would-be organ recipients – were in on the hoax and took part to raise awareness of the issue. *Big Donor* came perilously close to being the real article, though. It was only at the last minute, as the actress/donor was about to announce the winner that the presenter stepped in and gave the game away. *Big Donor* was used as a Trojan horse to make what is essentially a valid point: that people awaiting organ transplants have a very tough time of it. The point is certainly worth making, yet there are far better and more respectful ways of doing so – respectful of both the participants and the audience.

The values behind the show were based on relativistic thinking: it's OK to lie to the public, and to play games with peoples' health, as long as it's in a good cause. The ends justify the means. Lies are only harmful, says this line of thinking, if they're perpetrated in the pursuit of an evil cause. If you're trying to do a good thing, using dishonest means is perfectly acceptable. But was it really necessary to manipulate the emotions of the public before they would respond to the issue of organ donation? If the answer is 'yes', what does that say about our culture?

Do we *really* take note of significant problems only when they're represented in sensational ways, using shock treatment? Actually, I think most people are open to having their awareness raised on important issues and will respect those who try to do so without resorting to trickery. TV programmes like *Crime Stoppers* – and variations on the theme – have proven that people will take up a righteous cause if they're presented with facts in a responsible way. It seems we haven't completely lost our respect for the absolute values of the past, such as truthfulness.

The use of shock treatment is the cheapest way of attracting attention – and the least influential in the long-term. The problem with shocks is that to be effective they must become more shocking overtime. One generation's 'extreme' is often the next generation's 'mundane'. Who knows what form the next incarnation of *Big Donor* or *Big Brother* might take?

Right now, reality TV is often based on putting people together in extreme situations, where they are manipulated and emotionally exploited, and then capturing their responses on camera. Sadly, in their hunger for affirmation and celebrity, the 'players' agree to be handled in this way. Who's to say, though, that someday soon we might not find more entertainment value in turning the cameras on people who *haven't* consented to being filmed?

That's the fundamental problem with abandoning absolutes and embracing moral relativism: you're left with a world of shifting values where the most ruthless, cunning or manipulative will rule, because they're adept at shaping public opinion. By the way, here's my challenge to all the *Big Brother* fans out there: what kind of world do you want to live in ten years from now? What kind of media do you want pumping values into the next generation – say, to your own kids? What will you do now to set that in motion? Usually, the only sensible response to turning on shows like *Big Brother* is: *don't bother…*

Relativism Fails

Relativism can never provide a solid basis for our choices and values. It falls short because true freedom always presupposes a prescribed order. Within any group of people, individual liberties are based on our willingness to adhere to certain underlying conventions.

When you get into your car to drive to work, you don't consciously think about which side of the road you should be driving on. You automatically head off on one side of the road, right or left, depending on where you live in the world. You assume, without a second thought, that you can operate with freedom if you drive on that side of the road. What are you doing? You're submitting yourself to an underlying convention. If you applied a relativistic approach to the laws of the road – if you said, 'I'll drive wherever I want, thanks very much' – you'd be dead in no time.

Relativism fails because it relies on the incomplete wisdom of human beings. Let's face it: every one of us has at our disposal a very limited database of information on life. We can't see beyond our own experience. And even then, we tend to forget most of what we've experienced. If there are any reliable, universal principles to guide us through life, they must originate with someone who empathises with the human condition, yet whose understanding transcends ours. None of us – not even the most noble or far-sighted – can see far enough over the horizon to arrive, on our own, at a complete code of values that will never fail us or other people.

Several recent books have talked about the 'wisdom of crowds', the ability of groups of people to arrive at conclusions which individuals could never reach on their own. There is sometimes a collective wisdom in teams and societies that eludes us as individuals. Collective thinking, in the community, the workplace, the government and the family, can provide some startling outcomes. Yet there are plenty of examples in history of where the 'wisdom' of the crowd has proven to be less than wise, especially in the long-term.

I think it was Carl Jung who said that one of the reasons Hitler first rose to prominence in Germany is that he was the first person to tell the Germans what they were already thinking. Hitler articulated a deeply felt pain, anger and sense of injustice which came with the humiliation of World War I and its aftermath. For many Germans, the bond they developed with their *Fuhrer* in those early days stayed strong until near the end of the Second World War. Even when their beautiful and proud cities were being reduced to rubble, and persistent reports told of horrific goings-on in the internment camps, many people refused to entertain the idea that Hitler had failed them.

Of course, it wasn't until after the war that the full horror of the death camps emerged, but even then some people refused to accept that these evils were the work of their leader and his regime. The crowd was as blind as their leader; perhaps wilfully so. Many preferred to remain blind than to face what had been done in their name. This was just one example among thousands throughout history of what Jesus called the blind leading the blind, with both ending up in a ditch (Matthew 15:14). The writer of the Proverbs offered this insight: 'There is a way that seems right to a man, but in the end it leads to death' (Proverbs 14:12).

Not Everything Is Relative

If you want to make repairs to your car, you don't simply stick your head under the hood, play around a bit and then randomly pull out whichever piece of the engine is closest. You consult the manufacturer's manual; you look to the recorded wisdom of someone who knows this machine better than you, who knows the purpose and proper order of every working part. In a similar way, if you want to care for your life you can't just keep randomly doing whatever feels good at the time. You need to consult a higher authority; someone who knows how you were constructed.

Say 'moral absolutes' in these post-modern times and many people automatically assume that you're talking about random rules that are designed to stifle self-expression and stop them having any fun. Sadly, the negative way in which the church has sometimes communicated Christian morality has only strengthened that perception. As a result, in many parts of the world we have Christian music that nobody outside the church wants to hear, preachers nobody wants to listen to and churches that hardly anyone visits, except to take photographs as tourists! Christians have been shunted off into a small cultural ghetto on the periphery of mainstream society, in part because of a perception that anything that's Christian can't be much fun.

Contrary to popular belief, Bible absolutes are not based on the cultural tastes of killjoy Old Testament priests, or the mystical ruminations of out-of-touch prophets. They're certainly not founded on anything as flimsy as post-modern pragmatism or image. Their basis is the nature and character of God. Bible absolutes are based in righteousness, which says that the highest good we can do is to be like God in our attitudes and actions. When the Bible talks about morality, it doesn't point us to arbitrary rules; it directs us toward the character of God.

If you've spent more than five minutes talking to a professing atheist, you've no doubt heard the question: 'If there is a God, why is there so much evil in the world?' Actually, I think the opposite question is more illuminating: 'If there is *no* God, why is there so much *good* in the world?' If, as evolutionists would have us believe, we are nothing more than hunks of meat, without a spiritual nature, born out of chance processes and destined to have to compete just to survive; if all that's true, why do we continue to do good and often self-sacrificing things for each other? And why do we derive great joy and fulfilment from doing them? It's because we were created in God's image – and he is the essence of goodness.

The Bible says we should base our moral decisions on one question: 'If God is as the Bible describes him, how would *he* respond in my situation?' And the answer to that question can only be found in the process of revelation, where God makes himself known to us. As the theologians have it, the imminent cannot penetrate the transcendent – God must come to us, if we're to know him at all. The Bible's message is that he has done just that.

God's moral principles are not arbitrary and they're not given to smother our creativity. They are descriptions of what is real in God's universe. Everyday, we expect to have to obey the natural laws of physics. If we don't, we know there'll be consequences. The laws of physics are not laws in the normal, legal sense; nobody debated them, then wrote them down and instructed us to keep them. They are descriptions of the way things work in this physical universe. If you jump off your house, you will probably do yourself an injury. You can consult your lawyer all you want, but that won't change the law of gravity – because it wasn't instituted in a human court or parliament. It is a universal description of what's real, in a world that's governed by clear and unchanging natural principles.

We live in a *moral* universe too, one that is governed by moral principles. In this moral universe, truth is always exclusive of error. Something that is wrong can't become right, no matter how much we try to dress it up or how often we change its name. Moral laws show us how to avoid the kind of trouble which comes from breaking the ethical pattern that runs through the universe.

Thankfully, God hasn't left you and me to live up to his standards in our own strength. (Let's face it, most of us can't even live up to our own standards most of the time!) God sent his Son to cancel our moral debt; to give us a fresh start so that I can live well, as whole beings, in the power that he gives (Matthew 5:17). Now, we not only know the truth, we can live it out, so that it truly sets us free (John 8:32).

The Ten Big Ones

Consider for a moment what is arguably the most famous body of moral absolutes in the world, the Ten Commandments (see Exodus 20:1-18). These are more than arbitrary rules; they are reflections of the God who gave them. They each tell us something important about who he is and how he acts. In so doing, they describe the intended culture of the people of Israel who were called to reveal him to the world.

The commandments begin with: 'You shall have no other gods before me.' We are not to attribute to any lesser being – or any *thing* – the place of ultimate worship in our lives.

Today, we may not worship the household idols of ancient times, but we are inclined to give selfish interests, other people or material things a higher status in our lives than God. This, too, is idolatry. So is the holding of an idea above God. The ultimate act of idolatry may be saying that God does not exist, for this is a naked expression of pride. The atheist says, 'God, you don't exist. Why not? Because I say you don't – and there's no higher authority than me!'

Friedrich Nietzsche was born in 1844, near Leipzig. He possessed one of the keenest minds of his or any other age and became one of the most influential philosophers in history. Sadly, the bulk of his legacy was not one that lifted the human spirit; indirectly, his teaching contributed more to human suffering than that of perhaps any other mainstream philosopher.

This son of a Lutheran pastor, and grandson of Lutheran pastors on both sides of his family, announced that 'God is dead and we have killed him'. This triggered an entire 'God is dead' movement among liberal theologians in the nineteenth century. It also sowed the seeds of a denial of human worth, which led to massive human rights abuses in the first half of the twentieth century.

The historian Paul Johnson referred to Hitler, Stalin and Mussolini as the three devils of the twentieth century. Nietzsche's dogma influenced all of them. Nietzsche, with his abhorrence of all religions, and Christianity in particular, taught that we should abandon Christian virtues such as humility, compassion and mercy. These were signs of weakness, he said. We should instead seek to take the next step up the ladder of human evolution, striving to become the kind of superhuman race which was promised by a simple extension of Darwin's theories. You can understand, I think, why Nietzsche and his teaching appealed to Adolf Hitler, who revered the philosopher as a great man. Tony Campolo writes:

> 'If God is dead, as [Nietzsche] claimed, then evolution is the law of the universe. In such a universe, the most powerful survive, and the "will to power" is the basic human drive. Evolution suggests natural selection, in Darwin's terms, or the "survival of the fittest," in the words of Herbert Spencer. It is easy to twist such ideas into an ideology that justifies fascist values and to believe that the higher breed of humans are those who are able to conquer and dominate.'[5]

We may despise Nietzsche's core philosophy, but we might at least admire his consistency. Unlike most other philosophers of his time, he tried to live in line with his teaching, to personally follow it through to its practical conclusion. He pursued a lifestyle of rampant hedonism, spending much time and money on prostitutes and partying. In effect, he was living as if there is no God.

G. K. Chesterton wrote that to believe in the non-existence of God would be analogous to waking up one morning, looking in the mirror, and seeing nothing. Perhaps he had Nietzsche in mind when he wrote those words, for Nietzsche spent the last eleven years of his life in an asylum for the insane. His quest for meaning and love through sexual promiscuity had led him to contract syphilis which drove him mad.

Interestingly, Nietzsche himself prophesied what would come from his 'God is dead' idea. In The Real Face of Atheism, Ravi Zacharias writes:

> '[This] was Nietzsche's point: the consequences of the
> death of God would penetrate every avenue of life, and
> thought in and of itself would be unbearable. It could
> prove to be suicidal if man did not rise up and take
> charge. In fact, Nietzsche went on to say, because God
> had died in the nineteenth century, there would be two
> results in the twentieth century. First, he prognosticated
> that the twentieth century would become the bloodiest
> century in history and, second, that a universal madness
> would break out. He was right on both counts.'[6]

It is no accident that Europe, having left behind its pre-Enlightenment role as the great propagator of Christian truth, became the epicentre of two horrific world wars, which left more than 21 million people dead. As Malcolm Muggeridge once put it: 'If God is dead, something or someone is going to have to take his place. It will be megalomania or erotomania, the drive for power or the drive for pleasure...'[7] In twentieth century Europe, we saw the growth of both.

Holy, But Not Dull!

The first of the Ten Commandments reminds us that God exists and is the ultimate authority in everything. The second commandment springs from it: 'You shall not misuse the name of the LORD your God.' It reminds us that God is holy, and he expects that we will treat him with respect and reverence. I know, the word holy is not a popular one in our post-modern vocabulary, but perhaps we need to give it a second look. It might mean much more than we think.

In the book of Revelation, chapter four, we're given a preview into what we might call God's throne-room. In the apostle John's vision of heaven, there are special beings surrounding the throne of God. These are the highest of all the angelic beings who love and serve God. Each one possesses a beauty we can only wonder at; each has intelligence beyond our imagining. If any one of these beings was to appear before us, we would fall down in fear.

We would probably consider them to be gods in their own right, if we didn't know better.

These beings do nothing but gaze upon and celebrate the presence of God and, for all their majestic beauty and awesome intelligence, they find themselves reduced to almost one word, which they repeat over and over: 'Holy, Holy, Holy...' (Revelation 4:8).

In our culture, 'holy' has become synonymous with 'dull', but the angels of heaven know better: when you apply the word 'holy' to God it means anything *but* dull. It means that he is so far beyond what you were expecting, so much more than you are ready to handle, that his presence just takes your breath away and snatches the words right out of your mouth. You're left with just one word, which you utter almost reflexively: 'Holy'.

God's holiness refers to his separateness. He isn't like anything or anyone else; he is above and far superior to all that he has created, in heaven and on earth. No-one can compare with him for beauty, attractiveness, compassion, tenderness, justice, strength, power or any other positive attribute you can name. So, having any other god before him is, well, an exercise in futility and will lead us further away from all that's true. It's in our own interests to recognise God's uniqueness and to reflect this in our priorities.

What of the other commandments in the list? Why are we told to keep 'the Lord's day,' to maintain that one special day of the week for worship? Because God is a person of balance and order. Genesis records how he rested after his creative work. We must learn to do the same. As Jacques Ellul once put it, 'man does his work and God gives to this work its meaning, its value ... its truth, its life – and if God does not give this ... nothing remains of the work of man.' Without respect for God's sense of balance, without that one day for relaxation, relationships and reflection, our work quickly leads to stress, burn-out and low productivity.

Why should we honour our fathers and mothers? Because God is honourable and he honours those who respect him. Demonstrating respect for our parents in practical ways – that's what honouring means – it is a fundamental way of showing respect for the Father who gave them to us.

Why are we told not to kill our fellow human beings? Fundamentally, it's because God is a life-*giver*. Why should we avoid adultery? Because God is, by nature, faithful; he keeps his covenant promises. Why shouldn't we steal? Because God is totally honest. Why not testify falsely against someone else? Because God is truthful in all things and completely trustworthy; if he says something, you can 'take it to the bank'. And why not covet the property of others? Because there is no envy in the heart of God and knowing him inspires contentment.

Each commandment, each absolute, reveals and reflects the person of God. If we're to live up to our potential, we need to learn to copy him, to emulate the way he acts. The Ten Commandments were not given as life-enslaving rules, but as life-enriching principles, as statements that define a culture of life and blessing. If we treat them correctly, they add value to our existence – and most of the time we don't even need to be aware of their presence. Good laws never draw too much attention to themselves. They operate in the background of our lives, protecting us when we're in the right and gently warning us when we get close to the line.

Mohammed Ali reportedly boarded a plane one day, found his seat and laid back in it as far as he could, seat-belt unbuckled. As the time for take-off approached, the stewardess asked him to fasten his seatbelt. A few minutes later, she returned to find that he hadn't moved; his belt was dangling at the side of the seat. So, she repeated her instruction. A minute or so went by before she went by once more and saw that Ali hadn't moved a muscle.

'Sir,' she said, 'you really must do up your seatbelt – we're ready for take-off.'

'Ma'am,' replied Ali, 'Superman don't need no seatbelt!'

'Sir,' she replied, 'Superman don't need no *plane*!'

It's a good idea in life to know where our limitations lie! God's moral mandates are markers; they define the limitations for healthy living.

My homeland of Australia boasts some of the finest beaches in the world. The locals know, though, that if you want to enjoy a swim in safety, you must stay within the flags put out by the beach authorities. If you stray outside the markers, you're liable to become breakfast for a shark. Most of the time, swimmers only need pay scant attention to the markers; they're not really conscious of them, checking only every so often to ensure they're still in the safety zone.

God's laws are markers to show us where the moral safety zone starts and ends. In an unobtrusive way, they mark out the boundaries of a safe space, an environment in which we can enjoy life under his emotional and spiritual protection.

---

[1] *The Case for Faith*, Lee Strobel (Zondervan Publishing House, 2000), p. 80.

[2] *Christ and the Media*, Malcolm Muggeridge (Regent College Publishing, 2003), p. 57.

[3] 'Just say no – ministers about turn in drive to cut teenage prenancies' (*Sunday Telegraph*, October 15, 2006).

[4] *Christ and The Media*, Malcolm Muggeridge (Regent College Publishing, 2003), p. 46.

[5] *A Reasonable Faith: Responding to Secularism*, Tony Campolo (Word, 1983), p. 57.

[6] *The Real Face of Atheism,* Ravi Zacharias (Baker Books 2004), pp. 29-30.

[7] Quoted ibid., p. 32.

IDEA #3

SPIRITUAL ECLECTICISM
THE BEST RELIGION IS A MIXED RELIGION

We live in an eclectic age. People mix and match their clothing, to the point where you might say there's no such thing as a major fashion trend any more. People mix their media; with something from the worlds of TV, the internet, radio, the iPod and mobile streaming. Many do the same with religious belief or spirituality.

Religious eclecticism says the best religion is a mixed religion, that the only way to find a useful brand of spirituality is to combine the most attractive parts of all available religions. To find a religion that works, it says, you must shop around, then take the best ingredients from everything on offer and mix them together into a New Age soup.

Now, before we go any further let's be clear on one thing. Contrary to popular opinion, Christianity is *not* the only world faith that claims exclusivity. Muslims claim exclusivity, too – not just theologically, but linguistically. They believe that the consummate miracle of Islam is the Koran, but that this book is only truly recognisable in the original Arabic. Any translation makes it less sacred, so to really appreciate the Muslim faith to the full, you need a quite sophisticated knowledge of Arabic.

Buddhism is also exclusive. It was born when Buddha rejected two fundamental assertions of Hinduism – the ultimate authority of the Vedas, the Hindu scriptures, and the caste system. Hinduism itself refuses to compromise on the law of karma, the authority of the Vedas and reincarnation. Baha'ism claims to be embrace all religions, and in so doing excludes the exclusivists! Even atheists are exclusive: they dogmatically refuse to entertain the idea that God exists. You can't be an atheist *and* a believer in God. Yes, Christians are exclusive, but so are all the other faiths on offer.

The spiritual 'mix 'n' match' approach we see in the West

today borrows heavily from various traditions of mysticism, which divorce spiritual reality from material existence. Mysticism says that the only Jesus that matters is the Jesus of my experience. Whether or not Jesus was a real person, an historical figure, makes no difference. Perhaps he did exist, but wasn't as the Bible describes him. That doesn't matter either. All that counts is the spiritual concept that a Messiah figure represents. The subjective sense of mystery is all that counts – not the objective facts of history.

Religious eclecticism also borrows from Gnosticism. The Gnostics were a religious sect, a break-away from the early Christian church that flourished in the first two centuries after Christ. Gnostics taught that only those who are initiated into hidden, extra-biblical, spiritual knowledge can be saved. Predictably, they claimed to be the only possessors of this secret knowledge. They also believed that human beings possess a good spirit which is held inside a basically evil body. In their belief system, the body and the spirit are totally separate entities. As a result, we can do whatever we like with our bodies and it will not affect our spiritual lives, which are essentially good anyway.

The Gnostic sect operated more like an exclusive, ancient lodge than a true reflection of the wider Christian church. Yet its ideas are finding a new audience at the dawn of the twenty-first century, via the agency of the Gnostic pseudo-gospels.

What's In A Gospel?

The New Testament gospels – the word literally means 'good news' – are our primary source of factual information about the life of arguably the most remarkable and influential human being in history. In his entire adult life, this man travelled no more than 80 miles from his home town, which many archaeologists believed was home to no more than around 500 people. He had little or no formal education and no officially recognized position in any social structure. All of this is unremarkable for people of his time; but it *is* remarkable in someone who has influenced almost every major sphere of human affairs in the past 2000 years.

His public work and teaching, spread over just three years, changed the world more than that of any individual in history. Now, two millennia after his birth and ignominious death, people who say they have no time for him will often quote him or refer to the principles he espoused – often without admitting it and sometimes without realising it. His name, of course, was Jesus of Nazareth. He founded what has become the largest faith community in the world, with one third of the human race claiming to subscribe to it.

The gospels claim to give us eyewitness accounts of Jesus' ministry. Many historians agree that the last of them was completed by the late 60s or early 70s AD – certainly no later than 100 AD. Colin J. Hemer is a noted historian who specialises in the Roman Empire. He cites more than a dozen reasons why the book of Acts could not have been written after 62 AD, or about thirty years after Jesus' death.[1] The gospel of Luke was written sometime before this and if, as most scholars believe, the book of Mark was the first gospel to appear, it must have done so very close to the lifetime of Christ.

Relative to other ancient works of historical literature, the gospels were written remarkably soon after the events they describe – and, in some cases, within the lifetimes of people who would either have seen Jesus or heard of his ministry. They were produced and disseminated at a time when their veracity could easily have been challenged by contemporary people.

The earliest extant copies or fragments of our gospels date from as early as the middle of the first century – for example, the small fragment of Mark's gospel found in the caves at Qumran. Larger numbers of copies are available from the second and third centuries. In historical terms, our earliest copies are unusually close to the time of the originals. We also have a large number of early copies, which adds to their reliability.

Tacitus, the Roman historian, wrote his *Annals of Imperial Rome* in about 116 AD. His first six books exist today in just one manuscript, and it was copied in around 850 AD. There's a long gap between when Tacitus did his research and writing and the time of our earliest known copies.

Josephus, a Jewish historian of the first century, wrote an important history entitled *The Jewish War*. Now there are only nine Greek manuscripts of this work and they come from the tenth to twelfth centuries. Homer's *Iliad* was written in 800 BC and today we have less than 650 Greek manuscripts, which are fragmentary and were written in the second and third centuries AD – that's a long gap.

Compare this with the New Testament: in total, we have more than five thousand Greek manuscripts of the New Testament, or parts of it, on various materials. The first copies were written on papyrus, a very frail material. Yet we have 99 fragments of papyrus that contain passages or books of the New Testament. Some of these date to around 200 AD. We even have sections of John's gospel on papyrus that date to as early as 100 and 150 AD.

In content, these early copies are remarkably close to later versions which were used over the centuries by European translators. In fact, there are only a few very minor differences between all the copies found through the centuries. They are so small that no major Christian doctrine has ever been brought into question by them.

Sir Frederic Kenyon, former director of the British Museum, said that 'in no case is the interval of time between the composition of the book and the date of the earliest manuscripts so short as in that of the New Testament.' He concluded that, 'the last foundation for any doubt that the scriptures have come down to us substantially as they were written has now been removed.'[2] Scholars Norman Geisler and William Nix concur: 'The New Testament … has not only survived in more manuscripts than any other book from antiquity, but it has survived in a purer form than any other great book – a form that is 99.5 percent pure.'[3]

Some authorities have noted that there is more textual and historical evidence to support the accuracy of the four gospels than there is for any other works of antiquity: including Caesar's *Commentaries* and the works of Homer, Aristotle and Plato. New Testament scholar F. F. Bruce went so far as to say that, 'There is no body of ancient literature in the world which enjoys such a wealth of good textual attestation as the New Testament.'[4]

Taking Out The Trash

Almost from its inception, Christianity, like Judaism from which it sprang, was a 'religion of the book'; a faith based on written Scriptures. In the first centuries after Christ, spurious doctrines began to spread through some parts of the church. Many of them were contained in books that claimed apostolic authorship. The churches needed a clear statement about which writings were accepted as God's word and which were not.

Over the decades following the deaths of the apostles, the elders of various church congregations approved certain writings and rejected others. Some experts believe that by as early as 170 AD, most of the churches were in agreement as to which books were divinely inspired and which were not. They hadn't met to talk about it, but had approved much the same books independently, with only slight variations.

A short time later, leaders of groups of churches, who became known as bishops – literally, 'overseers' – started to formalise the selection of Christian books. Some critics will argue that these leaders sat behind closed doors in secret locations, passing around the proverbial hat and randomly picking out the names of New Testament books. Or that they simply chose the books they personally preferred, ignoring the wishes of the wider church membership. In fact, their work was strongly guided by the views of Christians throughout the known world. The choices they made were rooted in the historicity of the books themselves and their popular acceptance by the majority of churches.

There was no conspiracy of silence, where the church establishment tried to pull the wool over people's eyes. Nor was there a star chamber where a small coterie of leaders decided what everyone else should be made to believe.

Their message had proven its worth by changing lives for the better and helping Christians survive and thrive under the fiercest persecution. The message had been carried far and wide by the first missionaries, whose preaching often transformed whole cities – and it had been backed up with extraordinary miracles. Dr.

Bruce Metzger is a highly regarded academic at Princeton Theological Seminary and the author of many books on the text of the New Testament. He says:

> 'The canon is a list of authoritative books more than it is an authoritative list of books. These documents didn't derive their authority from being selected; each one had authorisation before anyone gathered them together... For somebody now to say that the canon emerged only after councils and synods made these pronouncements would be like saying, "Let's get several academies of musicians to make a pronouncement that the music of Bach and Beethoven is wonderful." ... We [already] know it because of sensitivity to what is good music and what is not. The same [is true] with the canon.'[5]

During the selection process, which went on for decades, a number of spurious books were left out of the New Testament canon – the word simply means 'rod' or 'ruler' and by inference, a measure. Among them were so-called 'gospels' which had been written by members of the Gnostic sect long after those of the New Testament – often under the name of one of the early church leaders. These included the Gospel of Philip, the Gospel of Thomas, the Gospel of Truth, the Apocalypse of Adam, the Acts of Peter and the Twelve Apostles, and the Apocryphon (or Secret Book, or Secret Revelation) of John, to name just a few.

While some of them contain interesting cultural information or religious ideas, the early churches rejected them from the canon of scripture for several reasons. For one thing, they were not written by eyewitnesses, or people who had been very close to eyewitnesses, as Mark was to Peter. They lacked the authority of the four New Testament gospels. They also contained teachings that were very different from those on which the church had been founded and through which it had grown so rapidly.

By the end of the fourth century, the church had basically agreed on a full list of New Testament books that it considered divinely inspired. Yet our four gospels seem to have been widely accepted long before that. In fact, they were generally accepted as early as 130 AD. We find them referred to in the writings of Papias, a church bishop, who died in 130 AD and they were mentioned by Justin Martyr in his *I Apology*, written around 155 AD.

Actually, the gospels weren't the first New Testament books to be written. The letters of the apostle Paul pre-date the gospels by some years. His writings are the earliest in the New Testament and in them he makes clear references to Jesus' teaching and key facts about Jesus' life – especially those surrounding his death and resurrection.

Because Paul wrote first, some people have tried to insist that the gospels were distortions of later history. The gospels, they claim, were written long after the time of the apostles, by people who'd been indoctrinated by Paul into believing that Christ was something more than a man. Sure, Jesus was a great person, they say, but a belief in his divinity was something added long after his death and propagated by Paul. Most serious scholars, Christian or not, now agree that this theory just doesn't fit the facts.

Within Paul's letters, for example, there are clear references to early Christian creeds and hymns. In 1 Corinthians chapter 15, Paul records what scholars believe was probably the first Christian creed. Christians may even have recited it when they met, as believers sometimes repeat prayers today. Paul wrote:

> 'For what I received I passed on to you as of first importance: that Christ died for our sins according to the Scriptures, that he was buried, that he was raised on the third day according to the Scriptures, and that he appeared to Peter, and then to the Twelve. After that, he appeared to more than five hundred of the brothers at the same time, most of whom are still living, though some have fallen asleep. Then he appeared to James, then to all the apostles…' (I Corinthians 15:3-7).

Most experts believe that Paul was writing this in 56 AD, just a couple of decades after the lifetime of Jesus. The creed he included was probably used in the churches for quite a while before that. Similarly, in Philippians chapter 2, Paul quotes what experts believe to be an early Christian hymn:

> *'[Jesus], being in very nature God, did not consider equality with God something to be grasped, but made himself nothing, taking the very nature of a servant, being made in human likeness. And being found in appearance as a man, he humbled himself and became obedient to death– even death on a cross! Therefore God exalted him to the highest place and gave him the name that is above every name, that at the name of Jesus every knee should bow, in heaven and on earth and under the earth, and every tongue confess that Jesus Christ is Lord, to the glory of God the Father' (Philippians 2:6-11).*

Paul wrote his Philippian letter in 62 AD, so the hymn it contains was in existence even earlier. All this points to a very early and wide acceptance of the essential elements of Christian doctrine which were later written into the gospels. The essential facts about Jesus – those relating to his death and resurrection – were already in wide circulation just a few years after he left the scene, as was the belief that he was the Son of God.

When Is A Gospel Not A Gospel?

The Gnostic gospels were also rejected for another reason: many of them presented a totally confused picture of God. According to some, the creator of the earth was not God but a lesser being who, trying to set himself up as God, acted rebelliously.

These 'wannabe' gospels were also laid aside because they did not accept Christ as the redeemer of fallen humanity. They emphasised instead the need for people to acquire the hidden knowledge only Gnostics possessed in order to be saved. In some cases, they suggested that Jesus was in need of redemption himself before he could redeem others. Although some of these apocryphal gospels record similar events to those in our gospels – for example, some of the statements of Jesus – the same books contain strains of pantheism and other ideas totally alien to the gospels.

The Gnostic gospels also possess none of the historical tone of the gospels. They were written in a fanciful way that is more akin to mythology than history. Most of our recent Gnostic revival has centred on writings included among the Nag Hammadi scrolls, which were discovered in central Egypt in 1945. The Gospel of Judas was among them. The sayings of Jesus we're offered in this book are devoid of any context: they're not grounded in any timeline of events. The New Testament gospels, on the other hand, locate Jesus' words and deeds in timelines of activity and in specific regions of Judea.

In the same group of scrolls we read of one writer who was purportedly transported back in time to Bethlehem at the moment of Jesus' birth, so that he could fill in for his readers the details missing from the gospels. We also see, in The Apocalypse of Adam, how another writer was transported back in time to the Garden of Eden, so that he could learn the speech of Adam and reveal what Adam taught after the fall.

Another source talks about Noah and his wife having major marriage problems. At one point, things get so bad that Noah's wife, in a fit of rage, burns the ark to the ground. Eventually, Noah rebuilds the ark and when the rains start to fall he closes the door just in time to keep his troublesome wife out. The same writer goes into great detail about Noah's wife having encounters with demons, which demand sex with her. These writers had no problem using bad history to sell a sensational story that 'tickled itching ears' – and a few modern authors have followed their example, as we'll see.

There's one more reason the Gnostic gospels were rejected: they often contain material that is totally incomprehensible – even, presumably, to the initiated! Take, as an example, the Gospel of Thomas which supposedly contains secret sayings of Jesus revealed only Thomas Didymus. Here are a few of them:

> 'Jesus said, "If your leaders say to you, 'Look, the (Father's) kingdom is in the sky,' then the birds of the sky will precede you. If they say to you, 'It is in the sea,' then the fish will precede you. Rather, the (Father's) kingdom is within you and it is outside you'" (Verse 3).

> 'The disciples said to Jesus, "Tell us, how will our end come?" Jesus said, "Have you found the beginning, then,

that you are looking for the end? You see, the end will be where the beginning is. Congratulations to the one who stands at the beginning: that one will know the end and will not taste death'" (Verse 18).

'Jesus said, "Congratulations to the one who came into being before coming into being. If you become my disciples and pay attention to my sayings, these stones will serve you. For there are five trees in Paradise for you; they do not change, summer or winter, and their leaves do not fall. Whoever knows them will not taste death'" (Verse 19).

'Jesus said, "Where there are three deities, they are divine. Where there are two or one, I am with that one'" (Verse 30).

Do you understand any of that? I can't. It carries none of the directness, clarity or power of Jesus' sayings in the gospels. I suppose that's the point, as the Gnostics were trying to sell a 'secret gospel' that could only be interpreted by the initiated. But this attitude has nothing in common with the spirit of Jesus. Yes, Jesus often taught the crowds in parables, later revealing the moral of the story to his disciples. Yet at times he seemed exasperated with the disciples' lack of understanding. After all, he said, if people are truly seeking God, they would get the message; it was clear enough.

Matthew's gospel tells us that 'the crowds were amazed at his teaching, because he taught as one who had authority, and not as their teachers of the law' (Matthew 7:28-29). Jesus can't have been too difficult to comprehend — the largely uneducated masses couldn't get enough of him. Sometimes they were so captivated by his teaching that they stayed with him for three days, forgetting even to go home for a meal (Matthew 15:32). I can't imagine they'd have felt that way if Jesus taught in the obscure terms given above.

From the same group of writings, we have the Gospel of Philip. Here are a couple of snippets:

'Christ came to ransom some, to save others, to redeem [still] others.'

'Light and Darkness, life and death, right and left, are brothers of one another. They are inseparable. Because of this neither are the good good, nor evil evil, nor is life life, nor death death.'

If you make a further study of these and similar Gnostic sources, you'll often find yourself wading through screeds of convoluted or incomprehensible material. The fact is, the exclusion of the Gnostic writings was not an arbitrary decision taken by a few obscure bishops. If anything, the Gnostic gospels excluded themselves!

The Dan Brown Con

There's a solid body of evidence suggesting that the New Testament gospels are accurate in what they say. Yet we periodically hear all kinds of wild theories that suggest the gospels might not have been telling the whole truth about Jesus. Most of these theories can be traced back to the Gnostics.

Recently, in Europe and the USA, we've seen a revival of interest in all things Gnostic. A plethora of TV productions and popular books have emerged, claiming to lift the veil on the Gnostic writings, reveal the real Jesus of history and, in the process, show how the church has tried to keep the truth hidden. Actually, these same claims have been made periodically right through history. In each case, there's been an initial stir – because human beings love a good conspiracy story – which is then followed by a massive loss of interest, as people discover these theories ignore the facts of history.

The recent revival of interest in all things Gnostic began with the novel The Da Vinci Code by Dan Brown.

Throughout the history of the Christian age, people have made their thirty pieces of silver by trying to discredit the historical facts about Jesus and especially the Easter story. Within days of the crucifixion of Christ, Roman and Jewish guards were paid to peddle a false tale surrounding the resurrection. Matthew records that they were paid 'a large sum of money' (Matthew 28:12). Their employers, avowed enemies of Jesus, needed to explain how the body of Christ came to leave its tomb while their guards had been watching over it. Only a few months later, false witnesses were paid to discredit the early Christian leader called Stephen. His powerful witness for Christ led to his death as the first Christian martyr. Money was involved in both of these murky affairs.

Perhaps the most infamous example of this kind of thing is found in the story of Judas Iscariot, the one-time disciple of Jesus betrayed his Lord for 30 pieces of silver. Dan Brown is just one in a long line of people, starting with Judas, who have either directly or indirectly tried to misrepresent, obscure or emasculate the power of Christ and his message.

Of course, betrayal is not the same as denial. Betrayal means turning on someone who has trusted you; it is made worse when that someone has been good to you. Judas was in many ways more culpable than someone like Dan Brown, for he had spent three years living day-in-day-out in close proximity to Jesus. Judas was an eye-witness to the remarkable goodness, healing power and uniquely humane teaching of this man from Nazareth. Jesus trusted him, even to the point of making him treasurer of his band of followers. Judas betrayed a friend to his enemies: a friend who turned out to be the most influential person in history. And he did it for the price of a small piece of land.

Mr. Brown, as far as I know, has never professed a Christian faith, so in one sense he can't be accused of a betrayal of Christianity. Yet he did betray truth, by suggesting that Jesus did not die as the Bible says, but went on living and eventually marrying Mary Magdalene, in spite of the fact that the gospels all describe Jesus' grisly death by crucifixion – as do several ancient historians of note.

For example, the first century historian Josephus – no particular friend of the early church – says in his *Antiquities*: 'Pilate, acting on information supplied by the chief men among us, condemned [Jesus] to the cross ... and the tribe of Christians, which has taken this name from him is not extinct even today.' Tacitus, writing a history of Rome in the latter half of the first century, also mentioned Jesus and his crucifixion.

Even ancient texts which were either unfriendly to Christianity or totally disinterested in it recognized the manner of Jesus' death and the passion of the early Christians' belief in his resurrection. The crucifixion is also attested to in some religious traditions outside of Christianity.

Dan Brown deliberately chose to overlook the witness of history, which reveals more extant documentary evidence for the life *and death* of Christ than for the person of Julius Caesar. Of course, Brown's book was a novel – in effect, a modern fairy-story. On that basis, his fantastic distortion of facts might normally be tolerated; he is after all a myth-maker. However, he claimed that the historical events he represented were based in fact. This was hubris of the worst kind.

No historian of any note has ever maintained that the death of Jesus by crucifixion is a myth. Even today, in our pluralistic and secular society, reputable historians might argue about what the crucifixion means, but they don't deny that Jesus died on a cross.

Historians were perhaps more annoyed with Dan Brown than anyone else. Many felt that by flying in the face of historical evidence Brown was reshaping people's perceptions about the past. Of course, it wasn't his lies about the cross that upset most of them; it was his misreading of the work and motives of people like Leonardo Da Vinci. A key part of Brown's plot was the idea that in his masterpiece *The Last Supper*, Da Vinci left coded messages about the 'real' story of Jesus.

The figure depicting St. John, says Brown, is actually a woman – a suggestion, by the way, which has been made in the past. Art historians are quick to point out, though, that Da Vinci often used aspects of the same human study on different characters in various paintings. One face might, for example, turn up several times in various works. Sometimes, a face might be that of a woman on a man's body or vice-versa. Da Vinci wasn't sending coded messages; he was simply being economical his best studies.

Ideas like Brown's have long been refuted by historians around the world and he knew it when he wrote *The Da Vinci Code*. Yes, it is just a novel, and in literary terms probably not a very good one, but when he insists it is based on facts, he is abusing the trust of his readership and misrepresenting history – and faith. All for money.

The one good thing about the popularity of stories like *The Da Vinci Code* is that it gave Christians a platform to share the real story of Easter. It gave us an opportunity to speak about the cross and resurrection to a previously disinterested crowd. At the end of the day, the crucifixion and resurrection of Jesus are such potent events in history that no mere novel can seriously challenge the onward march of the gospel. *The Da Vinci Code* may have been a temporary thorn in the side of faith, but like all false stories it is overshadowed by the power and efficacy of what Jesus did for us.

Gnostics At Nine

After *Da Vinci* and a few other novels had proven there was a market for neo-Gnostic conspiracy stories, several other writers jumped on the bandwagon, with all kinds of claims about the life of Jesus Christ. Then, because the worlds of entertainment, the arts and media tend to borrow so much from each other, TV producers also took up the same cause. Before long, major British and European TV companies were jumping at the chance to produce or broadcast documentaries based on the apocryphal Gnostic gospels. Many of them offered viewers little more than lightweight opinion which did more to titillate than illuminate, leaving behind more questions than answers.

More than one of the recent TV programmes featured the Gospel of Judas, which purports to give us the sayings of Jesus via Judas Iscariot. The traditional gospels all describe Judas as Jesus' betrayer. Prior to this act of infamy, Judas had been known to steal from the disciples' central funds, which Jesus partly used for the support of the poor (see John 12:6). According to the gospel that bears Judas' name, Jesus offered him a special place among the disciples, telling him that of all the disciples he alone would be taught the secrets leading to salvation. So, it says, Judas was not the black sheep of the group; he was a hero whose name has been unfairly besmirched by history.

Again, when it comes to Christianity in post-Enlightenment Europe, bad history is often used to sell a tall story. The record of history is in fact made to bow before the great god of 'good television'. In this worldview, proven wisdom must be polluted to suit more politically correct tastes, and worthy beliefs must be not just debated but brought into disrepute.

As a producer of TV programmes, I am proud of the fact that television has done much through the decades to help enlighten people about the life and cause of Christ. Even in a so-called post-Christian age, people remain fascinated with Jesus. To feed the interest, programme-makers have put together some brilliant pieces such as the BBC's *Son of God* series. However, there've been too many programmes that claim to be based on history, yet play again the same old discredited Gnostic themes: Jesus didn't die; he married a woman; they had children; their descendants are alive today. At that point, they leave behind the balance of historical scholarship and delve instead into tantalising conspiracy scenarios.

Almost invariably, these programmes end on a non-committal note. Having raised all manner of inconclusive theories, they meander around the desert of 'what ifs' before riding off into the sunset, leaving us to eat the dust of their confusion.

What makes these programmes bothersome and tiresome is the fact that they're presented by people we are led to believe are 'experts' of some kind. This is suggested either by virtue of their academic background, or simply by the fact that they look and sound good on the telly (and anyone who's made it onto the box must know a thing or too).

TV is incredibly influential today. My friend Joel Edwards, leader of the Evangelical Alliance in the UK, says, 'The reason the crowd around Jesus switched from "Hosanna" to "Crucify him" is that someone was manipulating the crowd. This is the role of much of the media today [and] the battle for the airwaves must be won!'[6]

Thank God there are many TV producers, writers, editors and commissioning editors who are committed Christians; they're working in a difficult but fascinating industry. Jesus remarked that though heaven and earth will pass away, the truth of his words will stand forever. At the end of history, even TV producers will bow the knee before the Lord of love and the Prince of peace and declare him Lord of all, worthy of our highest acclaim. I'm praying hard that many more will discover it before then.

In the midst of the renewed public interest in Gnostic traditions, there's a challenge for Christian leaders. We must give people confidence in the accuracy of the gospels, providing them with apologetic material that answers the claims of Gnostics and mystics. We must provide them with an apologetic *for* their faith, so they don't have to feel apologetic *about* their faith!

The gospels are reliable records of history; their writers are credible stewards of truth. A good example is Luke, author of the gospel bearing his name and the book of Acts. 'The general consensus of both liberal and conservative scholars is that Luke is very accurate as a historian,' says Dr. John McRay, professor of archaeology at Wheaton College. 'He's erudite, he's eloquent, ... he writes as an educated man, and archaeological discoveries are showing over and over again that Luke is accurate in what he has to say.'[7]

Modern archaeology has confirmed both the Old and New Testaments to a remarkable degree. The celebrated archaeologist William F. Albright writes: 'There can be no doubt that archaeology has confirmed the substantial historicity of the Old Testament tradition.'[8] Dr Norman Geisler, noted religious philosopher, says: 'There have been thousands – not hundreds – of archaeological finds in the Middle East that support the picture presented in the biblical record.'[9]

With reference to the New Testament, Geisler adds: 'Archaeology has confirmed not dozens, but hundreds and hundreds of details from the biblical account of the early church ... [including such small details as] which way the wind blows, how deep the water is a certain distance from shore, what kind of diseases a particular island had, the names of local officials and so forth.'[10]

When the gospel writers have proven themselves accurate recorders of the minutiae of everyday life in their world – including the climate, customs, diet, language and notable events of the day – why should we throw out their witness on bigger issues, such as the sayings and miracles of Jesus? The only reason to deny the latter is that Jesus doesn't suit out post-modern tastes, challenging as he does our perceived right to total self-determination. If he really is the Son of God, we may have to change our ways, or as he would put it, to 'repent'.

Critics have long railed against aspects of the gospel records, only to find that later archaeology has proven them accurate. For a long time, some historians scoffed at the idea of Pontius Pilate, whom the gospels describe as the governor of Judea at the time of Jesus' trial. He must have been a figment of someone's overactive imagination, said the cynics, because there was little evidence for him outside of the gospels – aside from a brief mention by Josephus. They persisted in this until not long ago, when a stone plinth was uncovered in the Judean region which bore the inscription 'Pontius Pilatos Procuratos' (Pontius Pilate, Governor).

Some have also mocked gospel accounts of the crucifixion narrative. For example, they asked, how could anyone seriously believe that darkness covered the entire region for several hours as Christ expired? Again, contemporary writers have backed up the gospel claims. Second century historian Julius Africanus wrote: 'On the whole world there pressed a most fearful darkness; and the rocks were rent by an earthquake, and many places in Judea and other districts were thrown down.' He goes on to cite the work of two other historians, Thallus and Phlegon, who also mention the same event. In his *Chronography XVIII,* the latter describes it this way: 'In the time of Tiberius Caesar, at full moon, there was a full eclipse of the sun from the sixth hour to the ninth.'

A full discussion of the historicity of the gospels is beyond the scope of this book, but there are many other sources that cover this ground. I especially recommend *The Case for Christ* and *The Case for Faith,* both by Lee Strobel, and *The New Evidence That Demands a Verdict* and *More Than a Carpenter,* both by Josh McDowell.

Which Compass?

Many people, thinking themselves tolerant, say that all religions lead to the same destination: it really doesn't matter what you believe, as long as you are sincere and don't hurt anyone else. After all, they say, surely the most important thing about religious belief is that it gets you to focus on something, *anything* bigger than yourself?

Actually, if two religious systems give very different answers to the basic questions of life, you can't say they're pointing in the same direction. If you hold two compasses and they give different readings about which way is north, you know that one of them is faulty. They can't both be right. As we've already seen, all the major religious systems of the world claim exclusivity at some level. Truth is, by nature, exclusive – and intolerant – of error.

Some people claim that it's impossible to test the claims of religious belief, because such claims rely entirely on subjective opinion. To a point, that's true. However, there is a sense in which we can measure the effectiveness or validity of a belief system through its impact on peoples' lives. To put it bluntly, does the religion do 'what it says on the can'? How has it affected the people who've accepted it? What has it done for them? How has it helped people develop, socially, emotionally and psychologically?

How has it impacted their society and culture? Has its influence overall been a positive one, leading to a more merciful, humane, equitable, peaceful and just society? How has the religion helped people in a material sense: has it helped them attain to new levels of material wellbeing? I'm not suggesting that religious faith should necessarily make everyone wealthy, but it should help people to aspire to something better, especially those who have little to begin with.

Has the religious system helped people on a physical level: does it offer hope in sickness, for example? These are all valid questions which can be applied to a religious belief system over long periods of history, as well as in contemporary life.

Historically, many things were done under the banner of 'Christendom' which were far from the heart of Christ. People have murdered and tortured each other in the name of Jesus, but even a hardened unbeliever will accept that nothing could be further from the *spirit* of Jesus. Overall, though, where true Christianity has been encouraged and allowed to flourish – not as a political entity, but as a deeply felt spiritual faith – it has often led to more open, compassionate, prosperous and just societies than those operating under different religious systems.

We can also test the claims of a religion by looking at the person, example and legacy of the founder. Who was the founder and what was he like? What did he say about himself; what claims did he make about his own identity and his special right to teach as he did? What did he offer to back up those claims? In the end, what right does he have to speak to me and my situation?

A test of any religious faith should include a look at the founder, but if you study all of the world's major religious systems you'll find that only Christianity stands or falls *completely* on the person of its founder. In fact, this was one of the cornerstone's of Christ's teaching. He ensured that we wouldn't be able to talk seriously about Christian faith without wrestling with the question not just of what he taught, but of who he was. This is summed up most succinctly in his declaration in John 14:6: 'I am the way and the truth and the life. No one comes to the Father except through me.'

C. S. Lewis was arguably Christianity's greatest twentieth century apologist, sharing his faith through children's fiction, sci-fi novels, essays and much more. As a young man, however, he was a professing atheist. At the age of seventeen, he wrote to a friend saying, 'I believe in no religion. There is absolutely no proof for any of them, and from a philosophical standpoint Christianity is not even the best.' Just fifteen years later, he was writing this: 'Christianity is God expressing himself through what we call "real things", namely the actual incarnation, crucifixion, and resurrection.'

After a long spiritual fight, Lewis had become what he described as 'the most reluctant convert in England'. He became a Christian, he said, because he just couldn't explain Jesus away.

Who Do You Say That I Am?

When we seek to discover the true identity of Jesus Christ we only have three options. The first is that he was a master liar. This, however, doesn't square with the moral integrity of his life. Think of the amazing people Jesus has inspired and empowered through the centuries. Consider what they have accomplished by keeping his teachings and following his example. Imagine, if you can, a world without Martin Luther King Jnr., or Mother Teresa of Calcutta. King's speeches and private letters are littered with references to both Old Testament prophecy and the life and teachings of Jesus. When you consider what Jesus taught, it's not surprising that one of history's greatest social reformers was also a minister of the gospel.

Mother Teresa often claimed that she had no interest in being called a social worker. First and foremost, she wanted to be known as a woman of God whose passion for the poor was born out of her love for Christ and her desire to serve him and follow his example.

People like these changed the world because of their willingness to try to live out Jesus' teachings. Yet as great as they were, their attempts were flawed by the usual human weaknesses – as they both attested. Jesus, however, lived out his own teaching to a degree that has not been seen before or since. In fact, it can be argued that no man ever lived out his own teaching so consistently and thoroughly as Jesus.

Jesus' enemies, if they could, would have pounced on any misstep on his part, quickly and gleefully exposing any gap between what he taught and how he lived. Yet even at his trial, when they were desperate to find grounds for his crucifixion, they were unable to find any fault in his behaviour and were reduced to paying people to bring false testimony against him.

Our second option is that Jesus was a deluded megalomaniac. Jesus clearly thought that he was the Messiah predicted by the Old Testament prophets. In a new and revolutionary twist, however, he saw the Messianic role as being the salvation of the entire human race and not just the Jews.

Consider, for example, the statement of Jesus in Matthew chapter 16. He asked his disciples who they thought he was. Peter answered with characteristic forthrightness: 'You are the Christ, the Son of the living God.' Any other Jewish rabbi would instantly have scolded Peter for uttering what amounted to blasphemy. No man could claim equality with God. Such was the Jewish fear of God that they dared not even say or write his name. They were so afraid of mispronouncing God's name, that if they were going to address God they would say something like, 'The Holy One, blessed be he'. They didn't use his personal name. In writing, they removed the vowels from his name, forming a kind of a code word, 'YHWH', which scholars now call the tetragrammatron and transliterate as 'Jehovah'.

Yet Jesus responded very differently to Peter's remark: 'Blessed are you,' he said, 'for this was not revealed to you by man, but by my Father in heaven' (Matthew 16:17). Clearly, Jesus was not of two minds when it came to his divinity.

Jesus often used very intimate terms in his way of speaking about God. Calling God your Father, in a very personal sense as Jesus did, was unheard of for the Jews – you just couldn't *be* that close to God. Yet in prayer Jesus sometimes went even further, replacing 'Father' with words like 'Abba' (Aramaic for 'daddy') which were more intimate – and he taught his disciples to do the same. Jesus was changing the rules for how people could relate to God. What kind of person can initiate this kind of new covenant with the Almighty? He must have thought he was someone very special indeed.

Some people have suggested that the concept of Jesus as saviour of the world was added some time after his death, that it wasn't a part of his teaching at all. This, however, ignores the clear documentary evidence of the eye-witnesses who spent three years by his side, listening to his every discourse. There are slightly different accounts of certain incidents in the gospels – or accounts that offer a unique perspective, reflecting the personalities of the authors. But all four of them clearly show that Jesus thought of himself as the unique Son of God who had come to rescue humanity.

One church historian has noted that references to Jesus as Lord and God are contained in the oldest Christian sermon, the oldest account of a Christian martyr, the oldest pagan report of the church and the oldest liturgical prayer (in I Corinthians 16:22). Clearly, adds this historian, 'the church believed and taught that "God" was an appropriate name for Jesus Christ.'[11]

Award-winning journalist Lee Strobel conducted an interview with theologian Dr. Ben Witherington. Asked who Jesus thought he was, Witherington replied:

> 'Jesus thought he was the person appointed by God to bring in the climactic saving act of God in human history. He believed he was the agent of God to carry that out — that he had been authorized by God, empowered by God, he spoke for God, and he was directed by God to do this task. So what Jesus said, God said. What Jesus did was the work of God...'

> 'Jesus believed he was on a divine mission, and the mission was to redeem the people of God. The implication was that the people were lost and that God had to do something — as he had always done — to intervene and set them back on the right track. But there was a difference this time. This was the last time. This was the last chance.'[12]

Was Jesus mentally unstable? It might seem reasonable enough on the surface; after all, mental institutions have seen their share of people who're clearly delusional. Yet the idea that Jesus was mentally ill simply doesn't fit with the sanity of his teaching or the positive impact of his life on history. Singer and social campaigner Bono was asked in an interview whether believing that Christ was the Son of God is farfetched. He replied:

> 'No, it's not farfetched to me.... I'm not joking here. The idea that the course of civilization for over half of the globe could have its fate changed and turned upside-down by a nutcase, for me, that's farfetched...'[13]

In the end, we're left with just one conclusion: that Jesus was who he claimed to be, the Son of God. C. S. Lewis summed this up succinctly in his seminal apologetic *Mere Christianity*:

> *'You must make your choice. Either [Jesus] was, and is, the Son of God: or a madman or something worse. You can shut Him up for a fool, you can spit on Him and kill Him as a demon; or you can fall at His feet and call Him Lord and God. But let us not come with any patronizing nonsense about His being a great human teacher. He has not left that open to us. He did not intend to.'[14]*

Bono echoes these thoughts:

> *'Look, the secular response to the Christ story always goes like this: he was a great prophet, obviously a very interesting guy... But actually Christ doesn't allow you that. He doesn't let you off that hook. Christ says, "No. I'm not saying I'm a prophet... I am God incarnate." And people say: "No, no, please, just be a prophet. A prophet we can take. You're a bit eccentric... but don't mention the 'M' word! Because, you know, we're gonna have to crucify you..."'[15]*

Today, neo-Gnostics try to discredit the historical Jesus, by making him into a conman and manipulator of history. The enemy of our souls knows the only way to destroy the Christian faith is by removing the objective basis for that faith – which is the person and ministry of Jesus. As in the past, however, the spurious claims of Gnosticism can be disproved by a careful examination of historical fact.

Designer God = No God

Neo-Gnosticism is the latest and most potent reflection of religious eclecticism, which raises far more questions than it answers. 'The search is everything,' says eclecticism. 'Make the most of the journey, because you'll never arrive at a firm destination.' The seeker after truth is doomed to go on forever searching, without any hope of finding.

Eclecticism of this kind results in 'designer religion', with a God who are is no longer a person to be known, loved, revered or enjoyed. He (or it) becomes nothing more than an impersonal force, a form of divinity you can approach like an abstract painting – it can be anything you want it to be.

Sadly, when people start believing in gods without personality, they lose their own sense of personhood. After all, if my gods, who are greater than me, must be all things to all men, then perhaps I must do the same. Perhaps I too must become an abstraction, living in a kind of moral and ethical limbo. This, of course, is the root of political correctness. The only way forward for human society, it says, is to remove all of the distinctives which separate one way of life from another. 'Let's just bring everything down to the lowest common denominator,' it says, 'extracting all the bright colours and reducing everything to a lifeless grey.'

Jesus Christ announced that God *is* a person we can know and love. He refuses to be 'all things to all people'. His truth is exclusive of error; yet his love is *inclusive* – he wants no-one to perish, but for all to entrust their lives to him.

Why is it important to understand Jesus? Because he presented us with knowledge about God that is quite unlike anything on offer from any other religious leader. More than any other religious leader or philosopher, Jesus answered the questions: 'What is God like?' and 'Is God interested in me?' Why is it important to recognise that Jesus' crucifixion was a real event of history? Because it was, according to Jesus, the climax of his work on earth, the ultimate act of God in rescuing fallen humanity.

Jesus lived, died and was raised in a real, historical context. He spoke into a real culture, addressing flesh-and-blood human beings at a specific time in history. If we over-spiritualise his life, as the Gnostics did; if we try to separate the historical Christ from some 'heavenly Christ', we lose sight of the greatest hope humanity has.

[1] See *The Case for Faith*, Lee Strobel (Zondervan Publishing House, 2000), p. 130.

[2] *The Case for Christ,* Lee Strobel (Zondervan, MobiPocket Reader format, 1998), p. 161.

[3] Ibid., p. 71.

[4] Ibid., p. 68.

[5] Ibid., p. 75.

[6] Speaking at the *Strategic Leadership Consultation*, hosted by Next Wave International, Spain, May 2007.

[7] *The Case for Christ*, Op. Cit., p. 111.

[8] *The Case for Faith*, Op. Cit., p. 129.

[9] Ibid., p. 128.

[10] Ibid., p. 129.

[11] Jaroslav Pelikan, quoted in *The Case for Christ,* Op. Cit., p. 161.

[12] Ibid., pp.161-162.

[13] *Bono on Bono, Conversations with Michka Assayas,* (Hodder & Stoughton, 2005), pp. 204-205.

[14] *Mere Christianity*, C. S. Lewis (MacMillan-Collier, 1960), pp. 55-56.

[15] *Bono on Bono*, Op. Cit., pp. 204-205.

IDEA #4

SOCIAL HUMANISM
THE HIGHEST RIGHTS ARE HUMAN RIGHTS

Social humanism says that the highest of all rights are human rights, which are the ultimate basis of a healthy society.

The church of 2020, the church of the near future, will be led by members of Generation-X and even more so by the generation known as the Millennials. This generation is more upbeat than Generation-X – largely as a result of the better nurturing they received as children – and passionately believes that, given the chance, it can build a better future. It is also a very large generation, with more members than even the huge Baby Boom generation.

Each generation is marked out by certain characteristics which reflect its shaping experiences. For example, Boomers (born somewhere between 1945 and 1961), are great idealists. They love to follow prophets who cry, 'I have a dream!' Their heroes are artists who sang anthems like *Imagine*. Boomers love to talk about vision.

Gen-Xers (born somewhere between 1962 and 1983) are great pragmatists. A major source of tension between them and the Boomers, especially when they're working together in teams, is that Gen-Xers want to move beyond the dream to figure out how it can be done. Their naturally cynical edge sets them up for a greater degree of results-oriented, strategic thinking. Meanwhile, Millennials (born between about 1984 and 2005) already show signs of a potential for great humanitarianism.

Like individual people, each generation has its own peculiar biographies. Each generation has been shaped by certain experiences in the period of its development and emerges from those early experiences with a particular cry of the heart. The Scriptures reveal a God who works through history in a generational way. If Christians are to bring about God's preferred future, they must do it in God's preferred way. To create the future he desires, God works through the heart cry of each generation, using it to move people forward in a certain direction. He connects the focus of their fervour to the gospel, through the church.

I've written elsewhere about the concerns and interests of Generation-X,[1] but the cry of a Millennial person's heart is: 'There's got to be more to life than my personal choices.' This is a generation that is *overwhelmed* by choice. Millennials have been surrounded by options since birth; they face almost unlimited choices about relatively insignificant things, like fashion and hairstyles.

Music plays a huge part in their lives, but it's no longer classified within a few broad categories, such as classical, jazz, blues and rock'n'roll. Every category contains a hundred subcategories, each with its own distinctive sound. Again, choices abound.

The same applies to much more important things like morality. Do you want to be 'straight' or 'gay', or perhaps even bisexual? It's your choice. Meanwhile, relatively new surgical techniques have put gender itself in the realm of personal choice.

In the midst of the maelstrom of choice, the Millennial generation cries out against boredom. In the mid-1990s, when first wave Millennials reached adolescence, the number one bestselling book among church-going youth in America was a little tome entitled *Jesus Freaks*. It was basically *Foxe's Book of Martyrs* repackaged for a new age, and it contained the same chilling stories of men and women, many of them young, who paid for their faith in blood.

At the time, I read about an American youth pastor who asked his large youth group to identify the spiritual gift they would most like God to bestow on them. Their top answer was the gift of martyrdom. The pastor said: 'I didn't even know there was such a gift! I certainly wasn't expecting that answer.' What does this say about the Millennial generation? It suggests that they long for costly purpose and the simplicity of living for a cause.

Studies have shown that many Millennials look to the future with a real belief in their ability to build great institutions and realign history for the better. Generally speaking, Millennials are much more optimistic about the future than Gen-Xers were at their age. This is a generation of team players, who want to cooperate with others of their age to build something significant.

The Millennial generation also embraces technology, but without any fuss. Boomers remember when the first pocket calculators hit the stores. Gen-Xers remember the first mass produced personal computers. But Millennials have never known a world without digital technology. For them, technology is not something to make a commotion about; it is simply a tool for getting things done. The rapid development of new technologies is normal and to be expected.

Generation X made Mr. Starbucks a multi-millionaire very quickly. The coffee shop provided the perfect milieu for young adult Gen-Xers to get together and provide for one another what they hadn't found at home – nurturing. When Millennials get together, they do so not to find nurturing, but to talk about what they can do together; they come together for participation, for involvement in something. They're perhaps the generation that is most attracted to projects promoting human rights.

Will The Real Gospel Please Stand Up?

As we've seen, God is at work within every generation, connecting the aspirations of the generation with the gospel of his kingdom. Predictably, Satan is also at work, attempting to sidetrack each generation, leading it away from its true God-given place in history into a position of compromise. He invites each generation to buy into a false gospel. In his letter to the first Christians in Galatia, the apostle Paul writes:

> *'I am astonished that you are so quickly deserting the one who called you by the grace of Christ and are turning to a different gospel -- which is really no gospel at all… But even if we or an angel from heaven should preach a gospel other than the one we preached to you, let him be eternally condemned' (Gal. 1:6-8).*

When Paul speaks of a gospel 'other than' the true gospel, he uses a Greek term that means 'beside, near to, or in close proximity to'. In other words, there are false gospels which might at first look like, smell like, feel like the real thing, but will ultimately prove to be phoney.

If the Christian church is to shape the future in a godly way, we must counter the false gospels within each major generation of influence – and especially with the generation that will carry the future on their shoulders. Social humanism, or the 'gospel of human rights', is a false gospel which is served up to a socially conscious generation like the Millennials, as a replacement for the gospel of the kingdom. And it is, in some points, quite close to the real thing. It falls down when it removes any discussion of God's gifts and God's rights.

Most of the talk we hear today about human rights doesn't go far enough. It doesn't, for example, remind us that human rights are a gift. The idea of human rights did not originate with treaties set up by UN or the EU. It didn't spring from essays by famous humanists, either.

Thomas Paine was a deist; that is, he believed in a supreme being who was in no way interested or involved in the affairs of the world he created. The God of the deist is removed from humanity; he has set the wheels of creation in motion and left them to turn as they will without intervention from him. In 1791, Paine wrote the first book on human rights. In it, he said that if we possess such rights, they must have been bequests from our Maker. They cannot be something we granted ourselves, he said. Thomas Jefferson echoed this when he wrote that 'all men are created equal' and 'endowed by their Creator with certain inalienable rights'.

The Genesis record shows that God gave us two fundamental gifts, aside from the gift of life itself. The first is dignity. Because we were made in God's image, have a special relationship with him and have been chosen as stewards of his creation, every one of us has the right to a life of freedom and respect. The other gift God bestowed on us was that of equality. There was no class system built into God's original order for humankind. God doesn't love one person over another; he 'does not show favouritism' (Acts 10:34). Every individual therefore has the right to equal respect; no powerful individual or group of people should impose their will on the weak. This is a theme to which the Old Testament prophets return over and over again.

What are the two fundamental bases of modern human rights law? They are dignity and equality. Each of these was a gift from God, yet he is most often left out of any discussion about human rights. According to the biblical worldview, with these gifts came a special responsibility and accountability, to each other and, more importantly, to God. The prophet Micah put it succinctly:

> 'He has showed you, O man, what is good. And what does the LORD require of you? To act justly and to love mercy and to walk humbly with your God' (Micah 6:8).

This is where human rights programmes often fall short; they are good as far as they go, but they present us with only a close approximation of what God intended. In the end, we can't have an effective protection of human rights without a sense of accountability to something higher than human rights.

You can see this with the history of Marxism and communism. In the beginning, many communists were driven by a strong moral passion, to give the downtrodden dignity and the poor equality. They were passionate about human rights. Yet communism in Europe became one of the saddest experiments in human history. In the end, it fell apart because it was morally bankrupt. Those who had promised to free the downtrodden had instead become their worst oppressors.

People who looked at communism through the lens of biblical revelation saw this coming. Communism failed because it tried to take up the first part of Micah's injunction, while ignoring the last. Acting justly requires a love of mercy, and that relies upon a willingness to walk humbly before God. Communism left God out of the picture altogether, believing as Marx famously put it: 'Religion is the opiate of the people.'

Some of the most effective human rights campaigners in our time have come from outside the world of politics. I admire the Bob Geldofs and Bonos of this world; people who will dare to speak up for those who wouldn't otherwise be heard. Of course, there are many thousands of people the world over who devote every day of their lives to help alleviate suffering. We don't see their photos in glossy magazines and they don't get to meet with world leaders. Yet they keep plugging away and for a great many of them it's because they feel a deep religious conviction – and especially a love for Jesus Christ.

The *Make Poverty History* campaign grew largely out of a movement called *Jubilee 2000*. Working in the 1990s, this coalition movement, involving people in more than 40 nations, called for the cancellation of unpayable third world debt by the year 2000. It was founded and driven by a group of Christian people who understood that social justice is a biblical mandate. They drew their inspiration not just from UN charters, but from the Old Testament teaching about the year of Jubilee.

During this special year in the calendar of Israel, all debts were cancelled and every debtor was released from prison. If someone had lost land through debt, it was returned to them (see Leviticus 25:10-55). Jubilee wasn't just about charity, or even aid. It meant correcting the unfair advantage which is present in so many debt situations and giving the 'little guy' a fresh opportunity for self-sufficiency. The members of *Jubilee 2000* understood that Jubilee still serves as a reminder of how God thinks, and how he expects us to behave. Actually, Jesus referred to it as being part of his *raison d'être*. At the beginning of his ministry, he declared:

> 'The Spirit of the Lord is on me, because he has anointed me to preach good news to the poor. He has sent me to proclaim freedom for the prisoners and recovery of sight for the blind, to release the oppressed, to proclaim the year of the Lord's favour' (Luke 4:18-19).

The Jews referred to Jubilee as 'the year of the Lord's favour', so Jesus was announcing that he came to restore Jubilee, first to Israel but then to every nation on earth. He wasn't necessarily talking about the legal practice of Jubilee, but the principle of favour on which it was built.

The members of *Jubilee 2000* took this idea seriously, believing that it placed upon people of faith a special responsibility for redressing social and economic imbalances. They asked Bono to be a part of their quest. He agreed and it was the beginning of a new level in his commitment to the struggle for equity. Again, his faith played an important part. He's often been quizzed about this in the media: what place does faith have in today's world? This is a typical answer:

> *'I look around at the twentieth century: it's not a great advertisement for unbelief... I will say this for the Judeo-Christian tradition: we have at least written into the DNA the idea that God created every man equal, and that love is at the heart of the Universe... The Greeks may have come up with democracy, but they had no intention of everyone having it. We have to conclude that the most access to equality in the world has come out of these ancient religious ideas.'[2]*

For Bono, Christian faith is central to a commitment to the poor and to human rights. Mother Teresa would have felt the same. In the midst of a bruising schedule which would leave most of us reeling, Mother Teresa set aside prescribed periods each day for quiet contemplation, meditation and thanksgiving. Whatever she and her co-workers happened to be doing among the desperately poor, they would drop everything for these precious times of quietness. She often credited these moments of communion with God for her ability to rise above the misery of her surroundings, with joy.

Mother Teresa became, in the minds of millions, one of the great champions of human rights. Yet it was not because of her commitment to a political ideology, but because of her deep love for God that she behaved so compassionately. She often reminded her co-workers that the only way we can render service to God is through our service of the needy. She proved that if we walk humbly with God, justice and mercy will flow naturally.

Any discussion of human rights that focuses on human justice and mercy alone represents a false gospel and won't go far enough to bring about lasting change. The gospel of God's kingdom is about justice and mercy flowing naturally out of a humble walk with God. Human rights arise out of God's rights. It is God's right to be worshipped as God and honoured as the giver of life. It is his right to be loved and adored as our Father in heaven, from whom we have received 'every good and perfect gift' (James 1:17).

When we give God his rights, when we assign to him the position he rightly deserves in our hearts, we become much better promoters of human rights. That's why Jesus linked the two greatest commandments: if you love God with all your heart, soul, mind and strength, you will love your neighbour as yourself. Christian, our challenge is not to criticise the efforts of others on behalf of human rights, but to put God back in the centre of human rights.

Every year, the organisation I lead hosts a summit for European church network and national ministry leaders. These specially invited 'leaders of leaders' come together from up to 20 nations for a unique round-table summit, called the Strategic Leadership Consultation. We discuss what Europe might look like in 10 to 15 years' time and what the church can and should do now to impact the future.

One of our recent guest contributors was the aforementioned Joel Edwards. Joel made many insightful observations about the spiritual condition of Europe and the opportunities before the church. One of the most memorable was this:

> 'We need to raise churches where citizenship is an issue. The early Christians were able to say to the Roman culture, which placed a high value on citizenship: "You don't want to kill us, because we are your best citizens!"'

As he said this, I began to imagine what an impression the church would make on major cities and cultures if every Christian set out to be a model citizen and every church invested in projects that promoted great citizenship.

I usually speak at many events to thousands of people in various corners of the world every year. One of the most innovative events I visited in 2006 was hosted by a friend of mine who pastors a very good church on one side of London. The event was called the Night of Honour and its aim was to celebrate people in the local area who had contributed something positive to the community; people who had demonstrated good citizenship. The church had sent voting cards through the post to thousands of people in the area, asking for their votes in a number of categories. Awards were given on the basis of the votes cast. There were awards for best carer working with the physically challenged, best school teacher, best youth worker and many more.

When my wife and I arrived at the event, we found ourselves walking down a red carpet which had been laid across the pavement and led into the church building. Inside, friendly and well dressed hosts waited to show people in. The event was run like a TV awards night – with real sparkle. As I watched the proceedings, waiting to speak, I was impressed by the fact that the event had attracted some of the most influential leaders in the community; leaders from the police force, city council, local schools and more. Why had they come to this event run by a church? Because the church was promoting and honouring great citizenship.

In *The Church of 2020* I wrote this:

'Jesus said that his followers were a "city set on a hill which cannot be hidden" (Matthew 5:14). We're not meant to be ignored. It's interesting that he said a "city" and not a club or an organisation. Why did Jesus use that word? I believe it might be because churches can represent, in microcosm, what their cities could look like under God – if people were to return to him and live by Kingdom values.'

'In most cases, one church working alone doesn't have either the numbers or the resources to change the culture of a city. But it can achieve this by working with like-minded churches across a city. Together they can say to the city: 'If you want to see what family life can be, look at us. If you want an example of how business can

be conducted with ethics and justice, look at us. If you want to see good leadership and government, where people willingly work together for positive common goals, follow our lead.[3]

Applying the idea of citizenship and the 'city on a hill' concept to the issue of human rights, the church could say to the powers-that-be in cities and nations: 'If you want to see what a proper response human rights can produce, look at us. We are the best human rights activists you have – because we understand the origins of human rights and their relationship to God's rights.'

If we're to influence the future of our cities and nations, we must begin to take the idea of missions beyond mere preaching. We must promote holistic Christianity; where mission is everything and everything is mission; where we don't compartmentalize the 'Christian' parts of life from the 'secular', so that we produce Christ-like fruit in every sphere of life.

I recently conducted a TV interview with Pastor Ray McCauley, social campaigner and leader of Rhema Family Church in Johannesburg, South Africa. The church currently numbers over 41,000 people and is still growing, but Pastor Ray's influence has extended far beyond the walls of the church, into the sporting, political and cultural life of his nation. I asked him how he sees the role of the church amidst all the challenges facing Africa today. He said this:

'People receive your truth when they see the quality of life it produces. Going into a squatter camp and delivering an evangelistic message is not what they need at that moment. They want to see us live out our Christianity. If we're going to talk about HIV, for example, they want to know whether we've got a home where people can die with dignity.'

'The most fulfilling thing in life is to be present in a place where your resources can actually meet needs.'[4]

For me, that is a wonderful description of good citizenship!

What an impact we would make on human rights, at home and abroad, if we all carried that thought through into action. We would emulate the great founder of the Salvation Army, William Booth. In his final sermon, delivered at the Royal Albert Hall a few months before he died in 1812, he said:

> 'While women weep as they do now, I'll fight; while little children go hungry, as they do now, I'll fight; while men go to prison, in and out, in and out, as they do now, I'll fight; while there is a drunkard left, while there is a poor lost girl upon the streets, while there remains one dark soul without the light of God, I'll fight - I'll fight to the very end.'

Booth believed in and promoted human rights long before the term had entered the popular discourse of Western cultures. Yet he was motivated first by his love and respect for God, and his desire to do as God's Son would do in his shoes. He showed justice and mercy because he tried to walking humbly with God.

---

[1] See *The Future is X,* Mal Fletcher (Next Wave International, 2005).

[2] *Bono on Bono, Conversations with Michka Assayas,* (Hodder & Stoughton, 2005), p. 207.

[3] *The Church of 2020,* Mal Fletcher (Next Wave International, 2006), p. 7.

[4] See the full interview at www.nextwaveonline.com.

IDEA #5

SCIENTIFIC EMPIRICISM
WHAT CAN'T BE PROVEN SCIENTIFICALLY
SHOULDN'T BE BELIEVED

Recently, I saw a TV documentary called *Bible Uncovered*, in which scientists looked at whether the miraculous events of the Bible could actually have occurred.

An archaeologist was asked whether the exodus of Israel from Egypt could have happened in the way depicted in the Bible. She responded: 'A lack of physical evidence tells me that the exodus never happened; or not the way the Bible describes it. And if you're Jew or a Christian, you shouldn't need to have scientific proof; because faith doesn't need proof.'

I suppose she meant well. She was trying to let people of faith down gently. 'It probably never happened,' she was saying, 'but bless your cotton socks for believing in it anyway. After all, it's not important that faith is based on anything factual. As long as it comforts you, that's alright. Whatever gets you through the night…'

This sort of thinking relegates faith to the realm of harmless eccentricity. It promotes a dualism which says that while science is concerned with 'facts', faith deals with 'tall stories'. According to scientific empiricism, scientific discovery is the only valid and reliable measure of truth. What can't be proven scientifically can't be reliably believed. A corollary of this is that science and faith are often seen as being opposed to each other.

In the wake of scientists like Darwin, many people have grown up thinking of science as the bastion of atheism and naturalism; a realm of thought that allows no space for belief in God. In 1937, German physicist Max Planck declared: 'Faith in miracles must yield ground, step by step, before the steady and firm advance of the forces of science, and its total defeat it is indubitably a mere matter of time.'[1] Some people still believe that to be true, but they are behind the times. Today, increasing numbers of scientists are swinging toward a theistic view of life. In many cases, they're replacing a belief in random evolution with the concept some have called 'intelligent design'. This is not necessarily the same as a belief in the creation story of Genesis; but it does hold that the incredible complexity of our universe suggests the work of a creator of some kind. Lee Strobel sums this up well:

> 'Darwinism can offer no credible theory for how life could have emerged naturally from nonliving chemicals. Earth's early atmosphere would have blocked the development of the building blocks of life, and assembling even the most primitive living matter would be so outrageously difficult that it absolutely could not have been the product of unguided or random processes. On the contrary, the vast amount of specific information contained inside every living cell – encoded in the four-letter chemical alphabet of DNA – strongly confirms the existence of an Intelligent Designer who was behind the miraculous creation of life.'[2]

Relatively new developments in science have pushed many scientists toward a belief in God, or at least a supreme power.

Isaac Newton, the father of modern physics, taught that the universe is infinite and eternal, and that was the general scientific consensus for a long time. In 1915, though, a defiant young scientist called Albert Einstein upset the apple cart when he published his work on the general theory of relativity. When applied to cosmology, his theory suggests that the universe is limited but unbounded; that it is spherical and expanding, like a gradually inflating balloon. As scientists have delved deeper into the mysteries of the universe, they've found that Einstein's paradigm seems to fit the observable facts better than Newton's. Now, if the universe is expanding, it is likely that there was a time when this process of expansion started.

The Big Bang theory is one relatively recent attempt to describe the beginning of all matter and to explain the expansion of the universe. It says that all the matter in the universe began with a microscopic ball of energy, which was heated to 100,000 degrees Celsius in a split second – that's far hotter than the centre of any star. This small mass became so compacted and hot that it exploded, which is when 98 percent of all matter in the universe was produced – in under three minutes. Huge energy was released, pushing the matter apart and the universe filled with light.

This theory has reinstated God as a real possibility in the minds of many cosmologists. Previously, many cosmologists had believed in the 'steady state' theory, which says that our universe is eternal, without beginning or end. The evidence now seems to point to our universe having a definite beginning, at a specific point in time.

Whatever begins to exist must have a cause, and if we take this argument far enough back, we must arrive at one great 'uncaused cause'. Something or someone had to set everything else in motion; something or someone who did not 'come into existence', who is eternal. That someone is God. He did not begin to exist – he never came into being – so he doesn't require a cause. He is, as Scripture says, 'the beginning and the end' (Revelation 22:13).

Some scientists have now gone a step further, saying that the development of life after the Big Bang was so improbable that it suggests the work of a guiding hand. Looking at what happened immediately after the Big Bang, one British physicist concluded that the odds *against* the initial conditions being right for the formation of stars – and without stars, we would have no planets or life – is a one followed by at least a thousand billion billion zeroes. He also estimated that if the strength of gravity were changed by just one part in a 10 followed by a 100 zeros, life could never have developed.[3]

In the end, even scientists who've been cynical about intelligent design have had to admit that many new developments point to the existence of God. Lee Strobel writes: 'Sir Fred Hoyle, who devised the steady state his theory of the universe to avoid the existence of God, eventually became a believer in an Intelligent Designer of the universe.'[4] Hoyle wrote a book entitled *The Intelligent Universe,* in which he said that the idea that life originated through some random arrangement of molecules is, 'as ridiculous and improbable as the proposition that a tornado blowing through a junkyard may assemble a Boeing 747.'[5]

Critics sometimes try to portray intelligent design as a relatively new concept within the scientific community, or one that's confined to a few scientific 'lightweights'. When you want to discredit someone's ideas, you might infer that they've not had time to be properly tested. In fact, many of science's greatest heroes through the centuries have believed in the existence of a higher power behind the natural universe.

Albert Einstein, winner of the Nobel Prize in 1921, wrote: 'Everyone who is seriously involved in the pursuit of science becomes convinced that a spirit is manifest in the laws of the universe – a spirit vastly superior to that of man, and one in the face of which we ... must feel humble.' Einstein believed, he said, in a 'God who reveals himself in the harmony of all that exists.'

Other scientists believed in the God of the Bible and took the Scriptures seriously; among them Kepler, Pascal, Boyle, Newton, Linnaeus, Faraday, Kelvin, Lister, Mendel and many others.

Darwin And Beyond

Of course, you can be a theist – someone who believes in a supreme being – and still accept evolution through natural selection. A supreme being could have sparked the process of evolution.

When Darwin wrote his first edition of *Origin of Species*, the 'bible' for evolutionary theory, even he maintained a belief in the existence of a higher power. In the earliest days of the development of his theory, he felt that someone or something had set in motion the whole process of evolution. This is something which is not often mentioned in the textbooks about evolution. It was only later, as his personal disillusionment with religious faith grew, that Darwin changed his writings to reflect a less theistic view of life. It was not scientific evidence that caused Charles Darwin to abandon belief in the existence of a higher power – and specifically the Christian God – it was simply a subjective, personal choice.

Christian apologist and philosopher Norman Geisler says: 'The evidence [for God] is there if people will be willing to see it. It's not for lack of evidence that people turn from God; it's from their pride or their will. God is not going to force anyone into the fold. Love never works coercively. It only works persuasively. And there's plenty of persuasive evidence there.'[6]

Many people today would describe themselves as theistic evolutionists. In many cases, these people are deists who hold that God is a nothing more than an impersonal force that is present in all things. This is the Luke Skywalker view of God: 'The force is with you, Luke.' Some people go a step further and claim to be Christians while holding to evolution, fully and completely as Darwin espoused it.

Actually, it is possible to believe that *micro*-evolution – evolution *within* a species – occurs and still be true to a Bible-based faith. It's hard to make a case that says that over time animals and plants haven't developed in different ways according to their environments. The family of dogs, for example, includes a great many different sub-families, some of which have developed incrementally over long periods of time. (I'm using the word 'family' in its common form here, not any scientific one, as scientists are still debating the proper definitions of many of their own terms.) Even today, we crossbreed dogs on the basis that it's possible to alter some characteristics through selection.

However, nature will allow only so much variation – beyond a certain point, mutations will kill. And to suggest that the dog as a unique life form originated from something very different to a dog is another matter.

I don't think it's possible, unless you totally torture and distort the scriptures, to accept the Bible and hold to a belief in *macro*-evolution, or evolution *between* species. The Genesis record doesn't say that, in the beginning, God directly created all the varieties of dog that we see around today. But it does say that he created living things according to their 'kind', which many scholars take to mean their broad species. Of course, it is further credit to the Creator that he made every living thing with the capacity to adjust to its environment over time – without becoming something completely different!

We've already seen how cosmology is leading many scientists toward the existence of God, but there is growing support for intelligent design from just about every other discipline of science. Take astronomy, for example. For much of the last 100 years, science has spoken about the earth as if it is probably just one of many planets that are capable of supporting life. However, many astronomers and geologists now believe that our planet is quite unique in our galaxy, and possibly the entire universe.

Astronomer Donald Brownlee and geologist Peter D. Ward write that, 'not only intelligent life, but even the simplest of animal life, is exceedingly rare in our galaxy and in the universe.'[7] Science educators Jimmy H. Davis and Harry L. Poe note that, 'rather than being one planet among billions, Earth now appears to be the uncommon Earth... The data imply that Earth may be the only planet "in the right place at the right time" [for life to occur].'[8]

At the same time, biologists are learning more about what they call 'irreducibly complex organisms', microscopic organisms in which the working of each part relies on the fully developed working of every other part. You can't break these organisms down into their constituent parts, because they need all of their parts to exist at all. How does this help the case for intelligent design? Simple: these organisms could not have come about as the result of a gradual evolutionary process. They can only have existed in their present form or not at all.

Scientists have now mapped the three billion codes of the human genome – a huge project, the results of which filled the equivalent of 75,490 pages of The New York Times. George Sim Johnson writes: 'Human DNA contains more organized information than the Encyclopaedia Britannica. If the full text of the encyclopaedia were to arrive in computer code from outer space, most people would regard this as proof of the existence of extraterrestrial intelligence. But when seen in nature, it is explained as the workings of random forces.'[9]

Then there is the suggestion of design from the study of the human psyche and human consciousness. Some experiments have suggested that human consciousness can continue after the brain has ceased to function. This indicates that the mind, the consciousness, is a separate entity to the physical brain. If nothing exists beyond time and matter, if no-one sits at the controls of the universe, we're left with a question: how did thinking, living, feeling, believing, conscious beings spring from mere natural matter which can do none of those things?

If, however, we introduce into the equation the idea of the mind of God, we have no problem explaining the mind of man. Philanthropist Sir John Templeton has asked: 'Would it not be strange if a universe without purpose accidentally created humans who are so obsessed with purpose?'

To embrace Darwin's theory, and the underlying worldview of naturalism, you need to believe that nothing produces everything; that non-life produces life and randomness produces fine-tuning. You must accept that chaos produces information, unconsciousness produces consciousness and non-reason produces reason. It's a very big ask!

Science, The Friend Of Faith

Modern science was born out of a Christian worldview, three centuries before the rise of Darwinism. As C. S. Lewis once pointed out, people became scientific because they expected law in nature and they expected law in nature because they believed in a lawmaker. In more recent times, at least since the Enlightenment, many scientists have tried to abandon the very thing on which science was founded. They're like people who've finished building their dream home, then try to rip up the foundations without disturbing the furniture!

True science has never been anti-faith. In fact, science seeks to answer completely different questions; it may be able to tell us how some things happen, but it can never tell us *why* these things are so. In an ideal world, theology and science would coexist in harmony, because each would know its own limitations. Where science would rely upon observation, theology would call upon revelation. In today's world, however, science attempts to overtake the role of theology, moving from a study of the physical to the metaphysical.

Sadly, theology often allows this to happen by equivocating on matters of great importance. When theology fails to give clear, concise and consistent answers to humanity's big questions, science moves in to fill the vacuum – even where it is not qualified to do so. This is not in science's best interests. The mixture of science with metaphysics produces pseudo-sciences such as astrology. The ancient Babylonians were highly sophisticated in their pursuit of science, but their science was weakened by an obsession with astrology.

Science is a God-given tool for the honest seeker after truth. It certainly can show us the wonder of all that God has made. The Psalmist may have lived in a pre-scientific age, but understood this very well:

> 'The heavens declare the glory of God; the skies proclaim the work of his hands. Day after day they pour forth speech; night after night they display knowledge' (Psalm 19:1-2).

James Tour is a nanoscientist and professor at Rice University and is on the cutting edge of research into the molecular world. He echoes the words of that Psalm when he says, 'I stand in awe of God because of what he is done through his creation. Only a rookie who knows nothing about science would say science takes away from faith. If you really study science, it will bring you closer to God.'[10]

Science can lead us to truth – but not the whole truth. Many things that are of core importance to human beings can never be discovered through the processes of natural science – because they are spiritual in nature. They can't be found simply through observation or experimentation; they require revelation, because they deal with matters beyond the natural world.

The writer of Ecclesiastes noted that, '[God] has set eternity in the hearts of men; yet they cannot fathom what God has done from beginning to end' (Eccl 3:11). God has limited our ability to understand certain things, without direct reference to him. He has made sure that we will need to rely upon him to reveal them. Is this because God feels insecure about sharing his knowledge with us? No, it is because he alone is the ultimate standard for all that is good, just, healthy, wholesome and pure. When we use our education and powers of observation without the protecting framework of revelation, we lose our ability to discern what we're really seeing, in the context of a holistic view of life.

Scientific philosopher Kenneth Kuhn correctly said that scientists don't base their judgements simply on facts; but on assumptions they make about the facts. He coined the word 'paradigm' to reflect the construct of reality a scientist builds to fit the facts as he or she sees them. According to the Bible, humanity's moral fall left our sense of perspective skewed away from truth, leaving us with an inner bias away from God. In that case, our paradigm of reality may sometimes be distorted even when the facts are staring us in the face. Yes, we are capable of great and noble works – we were, after all, created in God's image – but so much of how we see the world is affected by the fall. Our fallenness interferes with our ability to discern what is true in what we see. Unless, that is, we apply the truth that comes through revelation.

Without reference to revelation, our moral fallenness plays havoc with our application of knowledge, too. We end up with a world where, as Jacques Ellul pointed out, everything is means and there are no ends. Hardly anybody, in the midst of the many changes we are making to our world, stops to ask the big question, "Why?". Without revelation, education and observation produce only a world of technology without truth, mass communication without meaningful compassion and great wealth without good works. We can have all the learning we want, but without divine revelation we are prone to make terrible mistakes of judgement. Malcolm Muggeridge noted, with typical sharpness, that: 'The most highly educated society in Western Europe elected Hitler … need I say more?'[11]

Scientists Use Faith Too

Pure scientific empiricism says: 'What can't be proven can't be believed.' Biblical faith says: 'What can't be believed, can't be proven.'

In God's grand scheme, there are certain truths we cannot uncover unless we are willing to trust what we cannot see. Noah had to build a boat before he saw God's provision of protection through the flood. Abram had to leave his home before he could find God's Promised Land, and he had to change his name before he received his promised son. Joseph had to believe the dream he received as a teenager before he could rise to a place of influence. Daniel had to trust God's integrity before he could be rescued from a pit filled with ravenous lions.

To some scientists all this sounds like a religious mumbo jumbo. Yet, if we're honest, we will recognise that science also requires the application of a form of faith. Leading scientists recognise that major discoveries often come through processes other than observation and the application of logic. Albert Einstein said, 'the intellect has little to do on the road to discovery. There comes a leap of consciousness, call it intuition if you will, and the solution comes to you, and you don't know how or why.'

Religious people are not the only ones who exercise faith. Every scientific breakthrough comes because someone has believed something enough to set out to prove it. Scientists base their experiments on the assumptions they have made about reality. Faith in those assumptions drives the experimental process. A scientist cannot prove anything until he or she has first believed something. Faith is again at work, even if some scientists deny its presence.

Miracles: Only For Children?

In November 2006, the cover of *Wired* magazine – one of my favourites, normally – featured a headline which read, 'The New Atheism: No Heaven, No Hell, Just Science'. It featured an article about what it called 'the crusade against religion', which included a report on a conference in America devoted to all things atheistic.

It often amazes me how stridently atheists will defend, in absolute terms, a faith that claims there are no absolutes at all. Yet atheists are becoming more strident of late partly, I think, in response to a growing sense of spirituality in our society. One of the most outspoken evangelists for atheism is Richard Dawkins, the Oxford don who authored *The God Delusion*. He has written elsewhere that: 'The virgin birth, the Resurrection, the raising of Lazarus, even the Old Testament miracles, are all freely used for religious propaganda, and they are very effective with an audience of unsophisticated and children.'[12] Dawkins is a respected scientist, although he has made more of the name of himself through his atheism. But is he right: is belief in miracles something for little children and intellectual light weights only?

While Dawkins says he wants to debunk all religious belief, he reserves most of his criticism for Christianity in particular. And he has correctly identifies miracles as the crux of the Christian faith. The whole of the Bible narrative is filled with the miraculous. From God's creation of the cosmos with a single command, to the wonders produced by Old Testament prophets like Elijah, to the entirety of the life of Christ – miracles abound in the Bible. Critics like Dawkins will use this fact to set faith against science.

In fact, there is nothing particularly unscientific about a belief in miracles – as long, that is, as you accept that God exists. Dr William Lane Craig says: 'if there is a creator who designed and brought the universe into being, who sustains its existence moment by moment, who is responsible for the very natural laws that govern the physical world, then certainly it's rational to believe that the miraculous is possible.'[13]

A miracle is properly defined as an event that could not be produced by the natural causes operating at the time and place where the event occurs. There was nothing in the immediate environment to explain, for example, how Jesus could turn water into wine (John 2:1-11). Science can't reproduce this event; it is not open to experimentation. So, many will say that miracles like this one contradict science.

The truth is that while miracles might be said to exist outside of science, they are not contradictory to science. The goal of science is to seek natural explanations to phenomena we observe around us; miracles rely on unnatural occurrences, so they fall outside the coverage of natural science. But if God is the creator of the natural world, with its inbuilt laws, he can at any time intervene in the processes of nature. By definition, God can do anything that is consistent with his nature. He is not bound by the laws of time and space.

We can illustrate this point with an interesting analogy. The law of gravity says that if you drop an object, it will fall to the ground. But if an apple falls from a tree and you reach out to catch it before it hits the ground, you are not violating or negating a natural law; you're simply intervening. The law of gravity states what will happen in conditions where there are no natural or supernatural factors to intervene. Catching the apple doesn't overturn the law of gravity; it's just the intervention of someone who has free will and overrides the natural outcome. The law of gravity hasn't been overthrown just because you catch the apple.

Miracles work in the same way. God does not destroy or reverse natural laws when he works a miracle; he simply steps in at a given time and place to intervene in the normal course of events. Far from destroying natural processes, God's miracles often seem to extend or amplify them. For example, the turning of water to wine represents the speeding up of a process that occurs all the time in nature. Water falls as rain, which finds its way into the grape, which is later turned to wine. So, in effect, Jesus was speeding up a natural process.

In some cases, we might say that miracles of healing work the same way. The human body produces its own antibodies to kill intrusive bacteria and viruses. The body also has its own processes for repairing damaged cells. Some miracles of healing represent sped up versions of the same processes. When doctors treat illnesses, they try to get the body to heal itself, with a little help from outside. The difference with miracles is that the help comes from an invisible source, and the results often appear instantaneously.

Of course, the Bible describes different degrees of miracles. I mean, healing someone of leprosy is amazing, but it might not be in the same league as feeding 5000 people with a few loaves and fishes. And that can't compete with raising Lazarus from the dead, or the miracle of the Resurrection. The latter has rightly been called the miracle central to Christianity. Without the Resurrection, said the apostle Paul, Christians are no better off than anyone else and are 'to be pitied more than all men' (1 Corinthians 15:19). So, it's not difficult to see why this miracle is the one most often mocked by atheists.

Does believing in the resurrection of Jesus mean that one is unscientific, or against science, as the critics claim? Actually, the resurrection may be highly improbable – but that doesn't make it impossible, if you accept the existence of God. 'As improbable as the resurrection might seem to sceptics,' writes Lee Strobel, 'this has to be weighed against how improbable it would be to have all of the various to historical evidence for its occurrence if it never actually took place.'[14]

The improbability of the resurrection has to be set alongside the improbability of the empty tomb, Jesus' appearances to his followers, the sudden change in his disciples and the rapid growth of Christianity across the world soon after. In other words, if Jesus wasn't raised from the dead, you have to find a way to explain all the extraordinary events that took place at the time – remembering that the evidence points to the historical veracity of the gospels.

Logicians use a certain procedure when they seek to explain a body of observed data. They start out with what they call a 'pool of live options', a series of possible explanations for that data. Then, they choose which explanation best explains what has been observed. It's a bit like the old adage Sherlock Holmes used: if you eliminate the impossible, whatever is left, no matter how improbable, must be the truth.

Sadly, some sceptics refuse to allow supernatural explanations into the pool of live options. Because they are prejudiced against belief in God, they declare the improbable to be totally impossible. They refuse to accept that an event might have a supernatural explanation – even when that explanation best fits the facts.

This is strange when you consider the huge improbability of much of what goes on in the natural world. Sir Francis Crick, one of the discoverers of the structure of the DNA molecule said, 'the origin of life seems to be almost a miracle, so many are the conditions which would had to be satisfied to get it going.'[15]

Faith Is Not Superstition

Having said all this, it's not helpful to the cause of faith when people use belief in a superstitious way, or as a pretext for not investigating natural causes. That sort of thinking has often caused tension between the scientific community and members of the church.

Scientists will always – I think, rightly – challenge superstitious thinking. Why should we ignore the positive benefits of natural science and return to a time when everything bad that happened was seen as the result of supernatural forces? If you're a Christian, why would you want every bad thing – and especially every bad thing on a huge scale – to be called 'an act of God', when you know that this misrepresents him?

I like the story of Jesus healing the woman who had the issue of blood. The Scriptures tell us that she had spent all her income in medical bills, yet she grew progressively worse (Mark 5:26). In the end, the medicos of the time were unable to help. Jesus did not comment on her attempt to find relief through medicine – he certainly did not scold her it. He simply announced that her faith had healed her, and she received a miracle. There is nothing wrong with using natural science to better our situation, provided that we place our ultimate faith in God. Sometimes, even the best that science has to offer will fail to meet our need.

There is nothing inherent in Christian faith that makes the pursuit of scientific knowledge a waste of time. God is always honoured when human beings study the natural universe he has made, trying to improve their lot and that of their fellow man. It was, after all, God who told us to 'subdue the earth and have dominion over it' (Genesis 1:28). People of faith will often make use of natural technologies and techniques, just like everyone else, but with the added benefit of knowing to whom they should turn when natural solutions can't be found.

Friedrich Nietzsche reacted against the church, because he saw religion as nothing more than empty superstition. He ended his days alone and struggling for his sanity, having abandoned the faith of his father and grandfathers. I can't help but compare his end with that of the apostle Paul who, according to tradition, was beheaded in Rome after a life dedicated to preaching the miracle of new life in Christ.

After having been an outspoken and violent opponent of Christianity, he was converted through a visionary confrontation with the risen Christ. He then spent the rest of his days bearing witness to the resurrection, enduring all kinds of torture and brutality from enemies of the Cross. At the end of his life, though, facing imminent execution, Paul could look heavenward and say, with heartfelt passion:

> '[Despite my sufferings for the gospel] I am not ashamed, because I know whom I have believed, and am convinced that he is able to guard what I have entrusted to him for that day' (2 Timothy 1:12).

> 'I have fought the good fight, I have finished the race, I have kept the faith. Now there is in store for me the crown of righteousness, which the Lord, the righteous Judge, will award to me on that day – and not only to me, but also to all who have longed for his appearing' (2 Timothy 4:7-8).

---

[1] *The Case for Faith*, Lee Strobel (Zondervan Publishing House, 2000), p. 58.
[2] Ibid., p. 251.
[3] Ibid., p. 77.

[4] Ibid., p. 140.

[5] *The Real Face of Atheism*, Ravi Zacharias (Baker Books, 2004), p. 42.

[6] *The Case for Faith*, Op. Cit., p. 141.

[7] *The Case for a Creator,* Lee Strobel (Zondervan, 2004), p. 156.

[8] Ibid., p. 157.

[9] Ibid., p. 219.

[10] *The Case for Faith*, Op. Cit., p. 111.

[11] *The Very Best of Malcolm Muggeridge*, Edited by Ian Hunter (Hodder and Stoughton, 1998), p. 122.

[12] See *The Case for Faith*, Op. Cit., p. 57.

[13] Ibid., p. 61.

[14] Ibid., p. 66.

[15] Ibid., p. 100.

QUESTIONS FOR FURTHER STUDY

This section will help you get a clearer understanding of the issues raised in this book, especially if read in conjunction with the Recommended Reading and Recommended Viewing lists in the following pages.

Idea #1: Technological Pragmatism.
In what specific ways has technology improved our lives over the past century (give examples)? What major new technological breakthroughs are now on the horizon? What are the key ethical or moral issues raised by these emerging technologies? How can people of faith challenge a purely pragmatic outlook on life?

Idea #2: Moral Relativism.
In what specific spheres of life has relativism changed society's approach to morality and ethics? How have modern media promoted the cause of moral relativism and situation ethic? Give examples of TV shows or movies and discuss how they support a relativistic worldview. How can people of faith challenge relativistic living in a positive way, without becoming 'moral policemen and women'?

Idea #3: Spiritual Eclecticism.
Find examples in your world of where people are expressing a spiritually eclectic worldview. What are the historical bases for accepting the truth of the New Testament gospels? Why were Gnostic 'gospels' rejected by the early church? In what ways is Jesus Christ unique among the leaders and founders of world religions? What is unique about the Christian faith, in comparison to other world religions? How can one be truly tolerant without compromising one's central beliefs?

Idea #4: Social Humanism.
What are the historical origins of modern human rights law? How does a Christian outlook on life help in the search for human rights? Find examples in your world of where people are seeking dignity and equality. Find examples of Christian people, in modern times, who have lived out the mandate of Micah 6:8, and thus changed their

world for the better. How might Christian individuals and churches today practice the principles behind 'Jubilee'?

Idea #5: Scientific Empiricism.

Find specific examples of where contemporary study is nudging science toward a theistic view of the universe. Why do we say that science and faith are not opposed? What are the limitations of scientific knowledge? On what reasonable grounds can we accept the possibility of miracles? What are the differences between faith and superstition? How might individual Christians and churches demonstrate the reality of miracles, without becoming superstitious?

RECOMMENDED READING

The following books are recommended by Mal for further study on issues raised in this book:

The Case for Faith, Lee Strobel (Zondervan Publishing House, 2000).

The Real Face of Atheism, Ravi Zacharias (Baker Books, 2004).

The Case for a Creator, Lee Strobel (Zondervan, 2004).

Mere Christianity, C. S. Lewis (HarperCollins, 2001).

The Case for Christ, Lee Strobel (Zondervan, 1998).

Bono on Bono, Conversations with Michka Assayas, (Hodder & Stoughton, 2005).

Wild Hope, Tom Sine (Monarch, 1991).

Mustard Seed Vs McWorld, Tom Sine (Baker Books, 1999).

Understanding the Present: Science and the Soul of Modern Man, Bryan Appleyard (Pan Books 1992).

The Very Best of Malcolm Muggeridge, Edited by Ian Hunter (Hodder and Stoughton, 1998).

Issues Facing Christians Today, John Stott (Marshall Pickering, 1990).

FutureWise, Patrick Dixon (Profile Books, 2004).

New Evidence That Demands a Verdict, Josh McDowell ( )

More Than a Carpenter, Josh McDowell (Living Books, 1997 & 2004).

Answers to Tough Questions (sceptics ask about the Christian faith), Josh McDowell and Don Stewart (Living Books).

A Reasonable Faith, Tony Campolo (1995).

Reasonable Faith: Christian Truth and Apologetics, William Lane Craig (Crossway Books, 1994).

The Future is X, Mal Fletcher (Next Wave International, 2005).

The Church of 2020, Mal Fletcher (Next Wave International, 2006).

For more of Mal's extensive recommended reading list, on a variety of issues and subjects, visit: www.nextwaveonline.com.

RECOMMENDED VIEWING

The following online video files are recommended by Mal for further study on issues raised in this book:

Jesus Among Other Gods, EDGES with Mal Fletcher, 30 min. documentary, view at www.edges.tv

Moral Truth in an Age of Relativism, EDGES with Mal Fletcher, 30 min. documentary, view at www.edges.tv

The Art of Thinking, EDGES with Mal Fletcher, 30 min. documentary, view at www.edges.tv

Sex & Singleness, EDGES with Mal Fletcher, 30 min. documentary, view at www.edges.tv

Technology & Alienation, EDGES with Mal Fletcher, 30 min. documentary, view at www.edges.tv

Robotics, EDGES with Mal Fletcher, 30 min. documentary, view at www.edges.tv

The Genetics Revolution, EDGES with Mal Fletcher, 30 min. documentary, view at www.edges.tv

Fuelling the Future, EDGES with Mal Fletcher, 30 min. documentary, view at www.edges.tv

Warfare in the Age of Hi-Tech, EDGES with Mal Fletcher, 30 min. documentary, view at www.edges.tv

Mal Fletcher speaks with Winkie Pratney, 30 min. interview, view at www.nextwaveonline.com

Mal Fletcher speaks with Dr. Patrick Dixon, 30 min. interview, view at www.nextwaveonline.com

Mal Fletcher speaks with Pastor Ray McCauley, 30 min. interview, view at www.nextwaveonline.com

Mal Fletcher speaks with Dr. Tom Sine, 30 min. interview, view at www.nextwaveonline.com

Check out the many audio files containing topical messages by Mal, in the audio section at www.nextwaveonline.com.

Other Books by Mal Fletcher